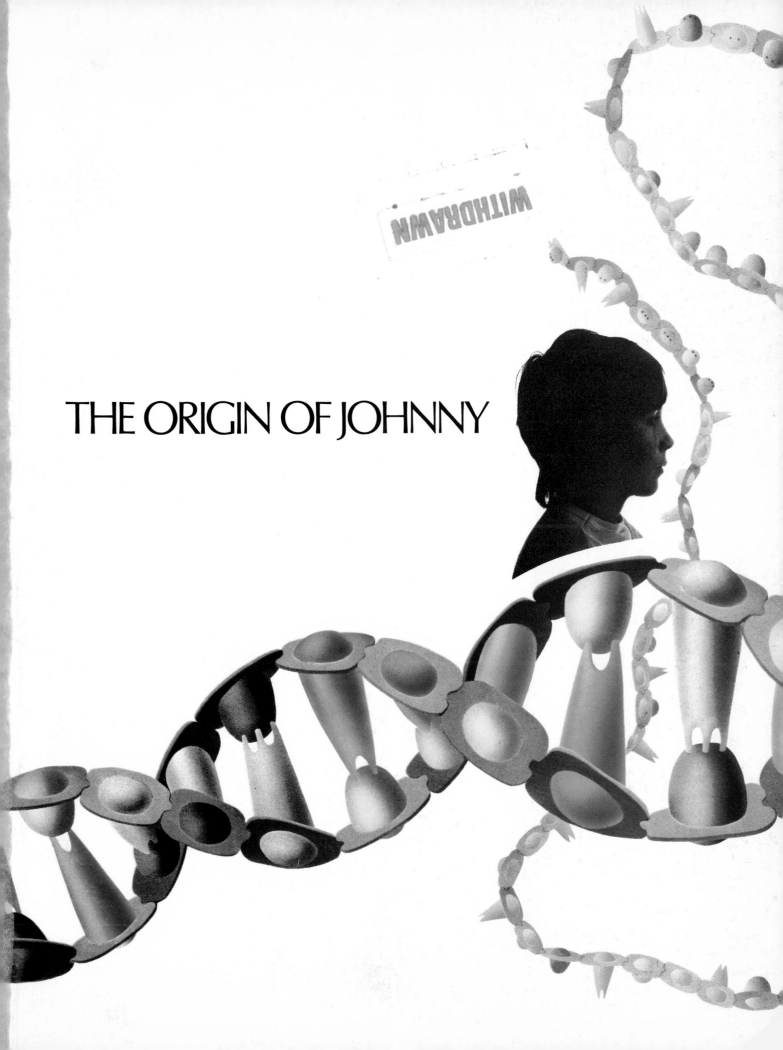

THE ORIGIN OF JOHNNY

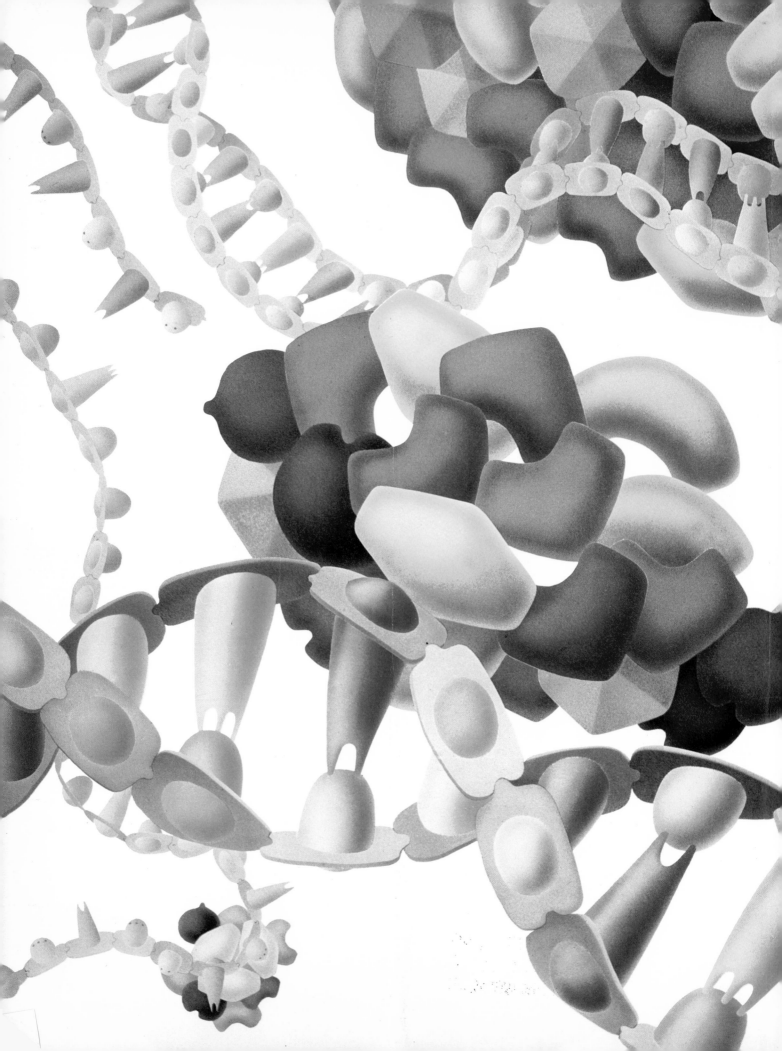

MALCOLM ROSS MACDONALD
Foreword by FRANCIS CRICK, FRS

THE ORIGIN OF JOHNNY

Alfred A. Knopf
New York, 1975

Many people have contributed to the creation of this book, and where it has been possible to define specific roles these are listed . Dorling Kindersley Limited would particularly like to thank Anthony Schulte whose support has been a constant encouragement, Richard Lewis who set the standard for the illustrations and painted many of them, and John Marshall and S.M. Groenbof who ensured that the illustrations were reproduced with matching excellence.

This is a Borzoi Book
published by Alfred A. Knopf, Inc.

Edited and designed by
Dorling Kindersley Limited,
29 King Street, London WC2

Managing editor	Christopher Davis
Art editor	Linda Nash
Text editor	David Reynolds
Artists	John Bavosi
	Claire Davies
	Jennifer Eachus
	Brian Froud
	Richard Lewis
	Sean Milne
	Graham Percy
	Allard Graphics
	Gilchrist Studios
Photographer	Michael Busselle
Johnny	Peter Sands
Consultants and Advisors	Lionel Bender, BSc
	Michael Boorer, BSc *Zoological Society of London*
	Ivor Evans, PhD *Department of Botany and Microbiology, University College London*
	Barbara Fenton, MA
	Peter Fenwick, MB, DPM *Institute of Psychiatry, University of London*
	Christopher Hill, PhD *British Museum (Natural History)*
	John Oates, PhD *New York Zoological Society*
	Christopher Stringer, PhD *British Museum (Natural History)*
	Hugh Tripp, PhD
Lithographic reproduction	L. Van Leer & Co. BV *Amsterdam*
Typesetting	Diagraphic Typesetters Limited *London*

Foreword

This book sets out to give answers to many of the most fundamental questions we can ask ourselves. In doing so it presents a fascinating introduction to several of the major themes of modern science–the origin of the universe, the origin of life, the formation of the continents and the relentless unending march of evolution leading to man, the unique animal. It sets man firmly in a chemical and biological framework while showing how his self-awareness and his complex culture place him apart from all other animals. The author graphically describes human embryonic development all the way from the act of love to the moment of birth and then sketches the complex process of a child growing up in an adult world.

From the lively text, helped by the very captivating illustrations, the reader learns of the vast size of the universe compared to his own familiar world, of the enormous stretches of time past and time to come compared to his own life span, and of the almost unimaginable complexity of living things, a complexity based on intricate, organized combinations of rather simple building blocks, the atoms and molecules of which we are made.

The book looks back into Johnny's past and depicts vividly how our recent knowledge has given man a radically new view of the universe and of himself, a view far more surprising, fascinating and awe-inspiring than those dusty fabrications of our hopes and fears conceived by earlier generations. But it also looks forward in showing how our present knowledge is incomplete; how in the future it must be both widened and deepened till we can see the universe and our own nature with far greater clarity then we do now.

This is an exciting story for any imaginative person but especially so for the young. In contrast to the uninspired way in which science is often taught in schools it is tremendously stimulating to see how these major themes can be communicated in a manner that is neither impossibly technical nor condescendingly simple. It is very refreshing that the author occasionally errs on the side of over-enthusiasm. Who can blame him?

I commend this truly imaginative presentation not only to Johnny but to all his family as well.

FRANCIS CRICK, FRS
Joint winner of the Nobel Prize in Medicine for the study of the molecular structure of DNA.

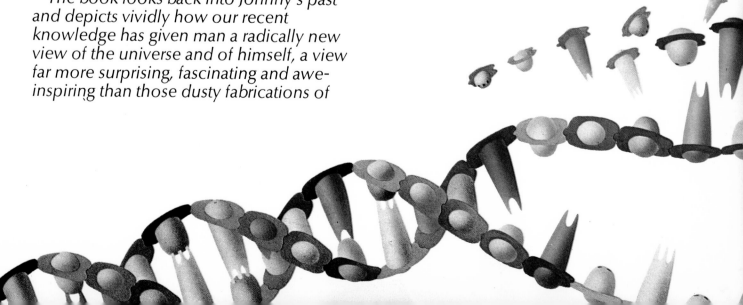

Who am I? Where did I come from? Where did everything come from? Each individual asks these questions at some point in his life. In fact man has been seeking his origin ever since he became aware of himself. And it is the ability to do this, to ask these questions, which makes him unique in the known universe, for, as far as we know, he is the only creature with his level of consciousness.

The answers have been many: intuitive, ingenious, fanciful. But now, in the scientific age, a vast amount of new information has become available.

example, and about aspects of the origin of life. And some startling discoveries have confirmed theories we already held. Notable among these was the discovery of DNA, the clue to the structure of all living matter.

We are still uncertain about our origins and possibly will never know the exact details of them. But, by using the current theories of science we can attempt to unfold a complete story.

That story reveals how man is an unbelievably complex rearrangement of the original matter of

Where do I come from?

The old explanations have been largely discredited, but since so much of the new information has been open to conflicting interpretations, no new all-embracing "genesis story" has replaced them.

This is partly because science has progressed unevenly; for instance, we know a great deal about physics and chemistry, but very little about biology, or time, or, much nearer to us, our own brains. In some fields we are beyond the twentieth century. In others we are still in the dark ages. Thus, it has been difficult to arrive at a coherent picture of our origins.

But, on the other hand, in very recent years some key theories have gained wide acceptance; theories about the origin of the universe, for

the universe; unique, so far as we can tell, in being able to demand an explanation for his existence, and unique *now* in being able to postulate a logical and consistent answer.

The story traces the matter that makes each one of us far back through time, back through the beginning of life, back through the formation of our planet, back through the birth of the stars, back to the very moment when the universe began. It also relates how that same matter, arranged in a living form, can be conceived and born, and mature into a conscious human being.

In this story that human being is called Johnny, but the origin of Johnny is the origin of all of us. Johnny's story is the story of the universe.

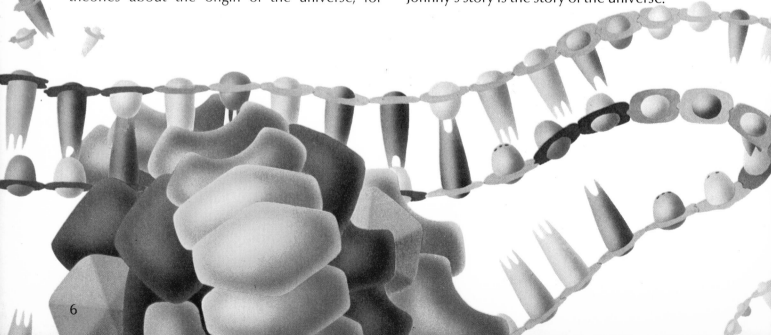

Before it began . . .

Before it began there was   , which we cannot know, nor can we name. But because we are human we cannot help trying to picture it: was not any thing, nor was it no thing. It had no middle and no boundary, neither inside nor outside. No height loomed over no deep, no light called to no dark, no warm answered to no cold. One part was totally like all other parts – and thus it could have no parts at all, nor numbers, nor degrees, nor differences of any kind whatsoever. So we have no name for it. And then suddenly there was a difference. There was both more than nothing and less than nothing, for which we have names: positive and negative, here and there, inside and outside, center and limit, start and end, matter and . . . And in that moment there was space. But that instantaneous space could not hold those numberless opposites, and in one mighty Bang they flew apart. And in that instant there was dimension and time as well.

Of all the matter launched forth in that gigantic Bang, only an infinitesimal part has drawn together to form the sun, the Earth, life and you. Nothing has been added, nothing removed. The materials for everything you have ever seen or touched were there. The materials for you were there, and those for me, and for this book. All are part of an endless ongoing process, a long sequence of rearrangements.

Still one unbeatable force links all those hurtling fragments, binding them into one system, one universe: gravity. From the moment of that mighty Bang until now, and from now until this universe ends, gravity has pulled and will go on pulling in its fight to reverse the expansion of the universe.

If gravity wins, and matter and energy return, time will have a stop and space will have but one point. Then, in one mighty Antibang, all may be annihilated and become, as it was before,   (which we still cannot know nor name).

Perhaps there is a super-universe in which this eighty-billion-year excursion from Bang to Antibang is no more than the crash of a single wave upon a rock in an unknown sea on a dead planet in the least-considered system, lost in the beyond, between the most paltry galaxies. If so, it cannot matter to us. Beyond the limits of time and space there is, for us, only silence.

In that instant when the universe began

In that instant, about 15 billion years ago, when the universe began it was a seething mass of blistering energy and short-lived particles of matter, all densely packed together at very high temperatures. This highly compressed globule expanded suddenly and hurtled outward at close to the speed of light. But as it expanded, its energy had to spread more thinly through ever larger volumes of space.

One hour after the Bang the temperature had fallen enough for stable particles to form – like protons, neutrons and electrons. But it was 10 million years before the expanding globule had cooled enough for these to form into stable partnerships or atoms. The first of these were hydrogen (1 proton and 1 electron) and helium (2 protons, 2 neutrons and 2 electrons). Soon all the universe was made of these two elements, rushing outward from the center.

But the formation of gas in the universe was not symmetrical. There were billions of places where its density changed a bit. The denser parts had a stronger gravitational pull than the rest – and naturally they became the centers toward which the less dense parts were attracted.

The universe, still expanding, turned into massed clusters of eddying gas, each a galaxy far vaster than anything we can ever imagine. Some were round, some elliptical, some irregular clouds of gas, and some, like our own galaxy, were flattened with spiraling arms.

Today the universe is literally immeasurable. To try to understand the size of it we have to use a "light year," the distance light travels, at 186,000 miles a second, in one year, which is 6 trillion miles. This is almost beyond the scope of our imagination, but to give some idea of the scale we are talking about, it takes 8 minutes for light from the sun to reach us, over 4 years for light from the nearest star to reach us, and 5 billion years for light from the farthest galaxy. And light from the most remote and mysterious objects in the universe, called "quasars," which are traveling away from us at almost the speed of light, has taken 12 billion years to reach us. So we can say that we now see these objects as they used to be 12 billion years ago.

Gigantic fusion factories

Our sun in the galaxy
Our sun is only one among 100 billion stars in our galaxy. It is situated about three-fifths of the way out. The galaxy rotates very slowly, completing a revolution every 200 million years.

Take 8 protons and 8 neutrons, and put 8 electrons whizzing around them, and you have oxygen. Take 26 protons, 30 neutrons and 26 electrons, and you have iron. 79 protons, 118 neutrons and 79 electrons make gold. There are 92 different elements made up in this way in nature, and apart from hydrogen and helium they have all been created since our galaxy formed.

In a galaxy there is a tendency for the whole mass to begin rotating. There is a tendency, too, for a disk to form that gradually grows more spherical towards its center. Within such disks you get subsidiary eddies, where local gravitational centers begin to pull in masses of gas and dust. These begin to form into a hundred billion whirlpools, every one the seedling of a star.

As the hydrogen and helium begin to concentrate, and as more and more gas is pulled in by the gravity of the growing star, and as the crowding and jostling of the atoms gets tighter and tighter, the temperature goes way off the end of any meaningful scale. Even the hydrogen and helium atoms rip apart, back to their constituent protons, neutrons and electrons. In places they are packed so densely that protons even fuse together with other protons.

This fusion happens only when the temperature is way up in the millions of degrees; but when it does happen it releases a massive amount of energy. How? It's a strange fact that two protons fused together weigh less than two separate ones. And four protons fused together weigh less than two pairs. The weight that is lost comes out as radiating energy – heat, light, x-rays and so on.

This energy-giving process of fusion is at the heart of the hydrogen bomb. So these stars are, in effect, natural hydrogen bombs – the force of the energy which would seek to tear the star apart, being countered by the immense pull of gravity.

But the hydrogen bomb effect will not last forever and all stars that are born have a "life" and finally die. Ordinary sized stars like our sun will last for about 10 billion years, but when the hydrogen "fuel" in the center is almost exhausted the star will become much brighter, a "red giant," hundreds of° times larger in size. When this happens to our sun about 5 billion years from now, the inner planets, including the Earth, will all be burned up.

This "red giant" stage does not last long. The remaining nuclear energy is quickly spent, and the star collapses under its own force of gravity. Its collapse continues until the entire mass is squeezed into a volume less than the size of the Earth. Such stars are called "white dwarfs." They are so dense that a bucketful of their material would weigh hundreds of tons. Slowly they radiate into space the last of their heat and fade into darkness.

But a different fate awaits a large star, many times bigger than our sun. The inward pressure of gravity is so strong that the star's interior burns quickly and the star dies very fast. When almost all the hydrogen is ripped apart the star collapses until its temperature reaches hundreds of millions of degrees. At this temperature the protons, neutrons and electrons combine to form those 92 elements. They are all made up in this way, all hammered together in the fiery heart of such stars.

The stupendous collapse creates energy so vast at the center that this gigantic fusion factory blows apart in what is called a supernova explosion, spraying its 92 elements into space, where they mingle with the existing hydrogen and helium gas. During the supernova explosion the star may be billions of times brighter than the sun and possibly as bright as all the other stars in the galaxy combined! Left behind is a "neutron" star of an incredible density, millions of times denser than the "white dwarf."

In really massive collapsing-star explosions the

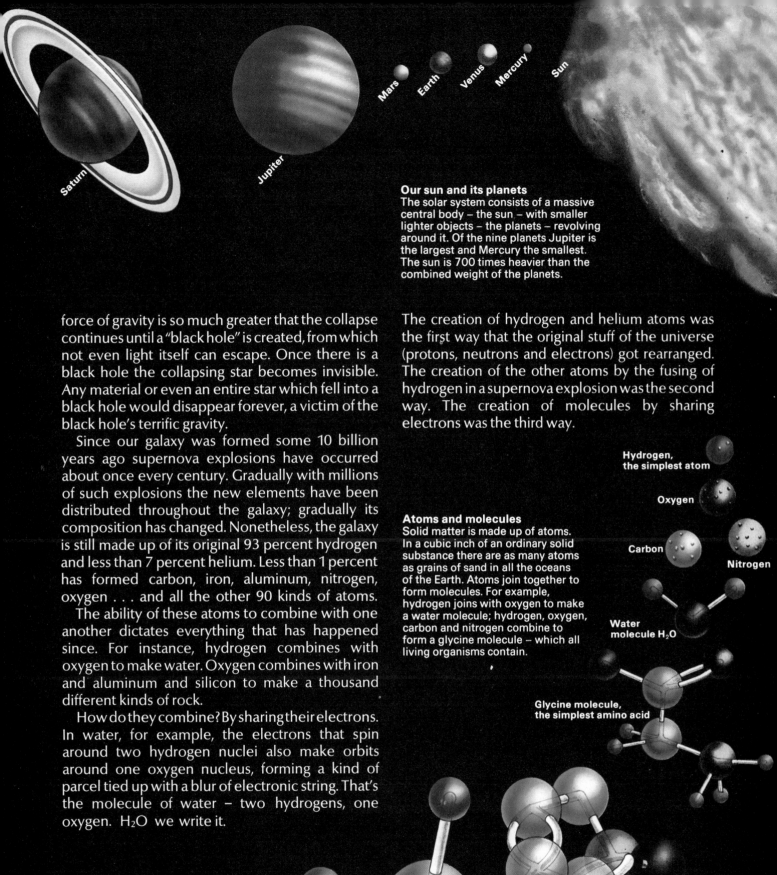

Our sun and its planets
The solar system consists of a massive central body – the sun – with smaller lighter objects – the planets – revolving around it. Of the nine planets Jupiter is the largest and Mercury the smallest. The sun is 700 times heavier than the combined weight of the planets.

force of gravity is so much greater that the collapse continues until a "black hole" is created, from which not even light itself can escape. Once there is a black hole the collapsing star becomes invisible. Any material or even an entire star which fell into a black hole would disappear forever, a victim of the black hole's terrific gravity.

Since our galaxy was formed some 10 billion years ago supernova explosions have occurred about once every century. Gradually with millions of such explosions the new elements have been distributed throughout the galaxy; gradually its composition has changed. Nonetheless, the galaxy is still made up of its original 93 percent hydrogen and less than 7 percent helium. Less than 1 percent has formed carbon, iron, aluminum, nitrogen, oxygen . . . and all the other 90 kinds of atoms.

The ability of these atoms to combine with one another dictates everything that has happened since. For instance, hydrogen combines with oxygen to make water. Oxygen combines with iron and aluminum and silicon to make a thousand different kinds of rock.

How do they combine? By sharing their electrons. In water, for example, the electrons that spin around two hydrogen nuclei also make orbits around one oxygen nucleus, forming a kind of parcel tied up with a blur of electronic string. That's the molecule of water – two hydrogens, one oxygen. H_2O we write it.

The creation of hydrogen and helium atoms was the first way that the original stuff of the universe (protons, neutrons and electrons) got rearranged. The creation of the other atoms by the fusing of hydrogen in a supernova explosion was the second way. The creation of molecules by sharing electrons was the third way.

Hydrogen,
the simplest atom

Oxygen

Carbon

Nitrogen

Atoms and molecules
Solid matter is made up of atoms. In a cubic inch of an ordinary solid substance there are as many atoms as grains of sand in all the oceans of the Earth. Atoms join together to form molecules. For example, hydrogen joins with oxygen to make a water molecule; hydrogen, oxygen, carbon and nitrogen combine to form a glycine molecule – which all living organisms contain.

Water
molecule H_2O

Glycine molecule,
the simplest amino acid

Amino acids
will join together to
form proteins

The birthplace of a hundred suns

It was about 5 billion years ago that enough large stars in our galaxy had been blown apart in supernova explosions to enrich the original hydrogen-helium mixture with a small fraction of all the other elements.

Imagine then some of that enriched gas swirling inward to form a gigantic cloud – the birthplace of hundreds of new stars. As the cloud grows tighter many separate swirling eddies form; and one of these is the embryo sun. As the gas and dust come together under the influence of gravity, the inner part of the eddy pulls together to form the sun, which begins to rotate at greater and greater speeds. This rapid rotation causes the outer part to flatten into an immense disk over a billion miles wide–here the earth and planets will form.

As the heat builds up in the sun's core it begins to glow dimly, but later, when nuclear reactions set in, the temperature rockets to a staggering 14 million degrees. Our sun is now ablaze and mature. Very little will change in the next 10 billion years.

When all the stars in that gigantic cloud have formed, they slowly begin to drift apart to their present distances. Many stars like our sun must have been born – many that would be stable enough to support life on their nearby planets.

The sun is a very ordinary star in our galaxy, but it is nevertheless an amazing body. 860,000 miles in diameter, it never ceases to radiate 370,000 billion billion kilowatts of energy out into space. The Earth absorbs only one two billionth part of that energy. And yet that is two million times the present energy requirements of mankind.

Dust into grains, pebbles into planets

Think back to that vast disk stretching more than a billion miles around the early sun. Small eddies have formed there and the heavier elements have gathered into solid matter; the dust has turned into grains, the grains into pebbles, and the pebbles into boulders.

So it was a very lumpy sort of debris – with some lumps the size of mountains – that finally converged on points at varying distances from the sun. As these pebbles and monster boulders collapsed on one another under gravitation, they formed into still larger bodies – the planets.

As the planets were forming, the infant sun began to slow down to its present speed and literally let go of the lighter elements in the disk, which were hydrogen and helium. But the sun itself is massive enough to retain all its own constituents, and if you make an allowance for the small amount of hydrogen it has since converted into helium – the process that produces all the sun's vast outpouring of energy – its composition was very close to that enriched gas and dust of the galaxy: 93 percent hydrogen, less than 7 percent helium, less than 1 percent everything else.

The outer planets – Jupiter, Saturn, Uranus and Neptune – are giants and therefore more massive than the smaller ones. Greater mass gives greater gravitational pull and this has enabled them to hold on to almost all of their hydrogen and helium. In fact Jupiter is almost a star. But although the most massive, the inward force of its gravitation is still not enough to set up the "hydrogen bomb" effect.

The inner planets – Mercury, Venus, Earth and Mars – are smaller and have a weaker gravitational pull; so they quickly lose a great deal of the two lighter gases. By contrast, they tend to retain all the heavier elements – carbon, iron, nitrogen, aluminum, and so on.

There are two other forms of planet. The asteroids, the great ring of boulders between Mars and Jupiter, may be a planet that broke up; and Pluto, the most remote of all the planets, may be a moon that got away from Neptune. About the size of Mercury, it swings round the sun in a very elongated orbit.

To support life a planet must be a certain distance from the sun. Too near and the atmosphere boils off into space; too far and it freezes – especially the water vapor, which is essential to our kind of life.

Only the Earth is so positioned.

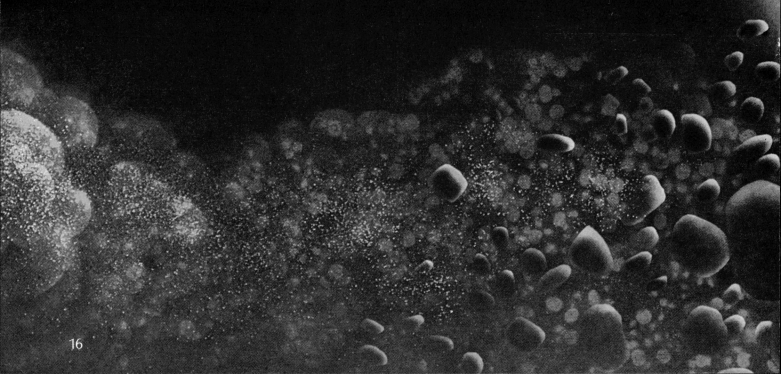

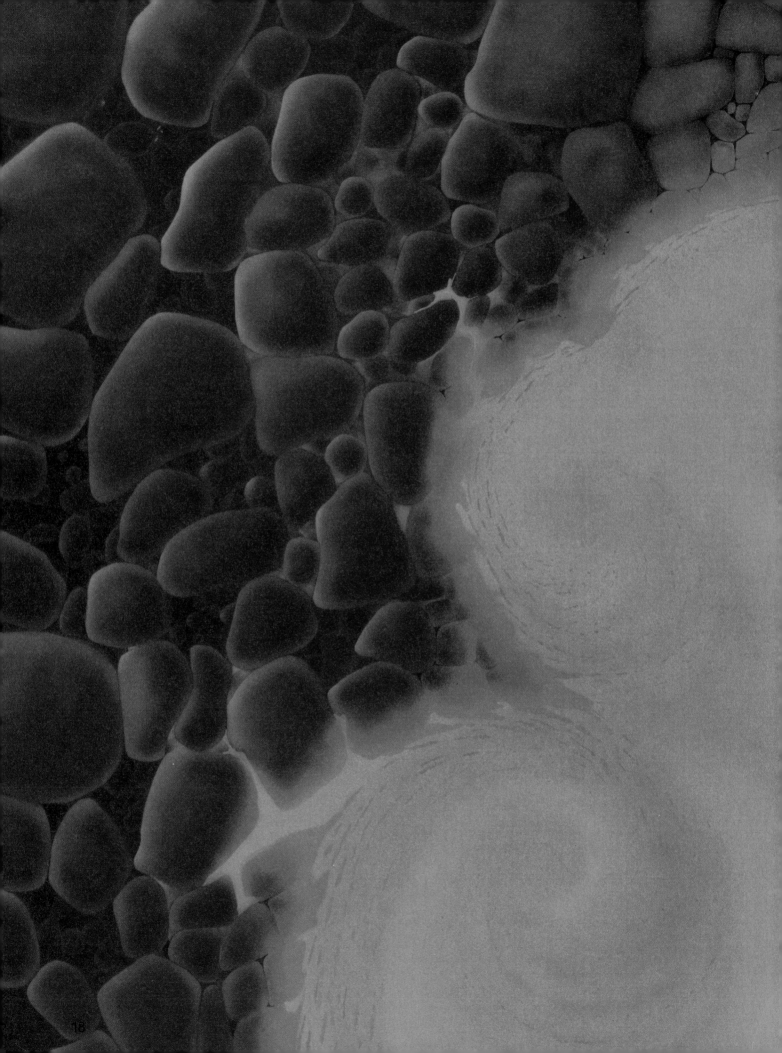

The whole Earth very nearly melted

The Earth, when it formed, was colder and more solid than it has ever been since. No earthquakes, no volcanoes, no oceans. Just cold dust and cold pebbles and cold boulders.

But as they crashed together and grew into ever larger masses, their sheer bulk and friction began to heat them up. Also, locked inside the growing bulk were atoms of uranium, thorium, radium – big, unstable atoms that can split up spontaneously and in their millions release vast jolts of nuclear energy. That same energy, now trapped deep in the bowels of the ever-growing Earth, began to heat it up. Indeed, it provided so much heat that the whole Earth very nearly melted.

It certainly melted the rock again. When this happened, the different constituents locked in the rock were free to move. The two main ones were iron, which is heavy, and silicon, which is light. The heavy iron sank to the core, taking with it things like nickel, platinum and gold. The lighter silicon floated up to the surface, bringing with it even heavy elements like lead and uranium, which have a chemical liking for silicon.

And then the outer part of the core – the mantle – cooled and turned solid, beginning with a mass of iron, silicon and oxygen minerals. In giant crystals they sank down about 220 miles, where they came to rest, floating on the surface of the even heavier (and still molten) core of nickel-iron minerals, 3600 miles across. Like the ice in a glacier, you could say that this mantle is solid, but under all that heat and pressure it can actually flow in a plastic sort of way.

Next to harden were the basalt minerals – iron oxides and compounds of aluminum and silicon. They settled in a thin, five-mile-deep crust around the globe. All that was left then was granite, the lightest rock on the primitive Earth. There wasn't enough of it to form a complete skin on top of the crust. In fact, granite covered only about one-third of the globe, perhaps in one big raft, perhaps in several smaller ones.

This new arrangement may have been stable for a while, but it could not last long. Those splitting atoms were still heating up the innards of the Earth, turning it into one vast chemical cauldron and building up stresses that soon would tear great cracks in the crust and rip holes in the skin. Down in that cauldron new gases were cooking. Methane, made of carbon and hydrogen; ammonia, made of nitrogen and hydrogen; carbon dioxide, made of carbon and oxygen; and water, raised to the temperature of superhot steam.

Forget the gases; but look at what they are made of: carbon, hydrogen, nitrogen and oxygen – vital elements in the next great rearrangement of matter, to us the most stupendous one of all. The beginning of life itself. And here they are now, belching forth from a hundred thousand volcanoes, rushing out to form an atmosphere. No longer locked away in rock and crystals, but in gases where each molecule is free to rush hither and thither and react with others – once the Earth has cooled enough for the steam to condense into clouds, and for the clouds to condense into raindrops. Before life can begin rain falls ceaselessly for thousands of years creating lakes, seas and oceans.

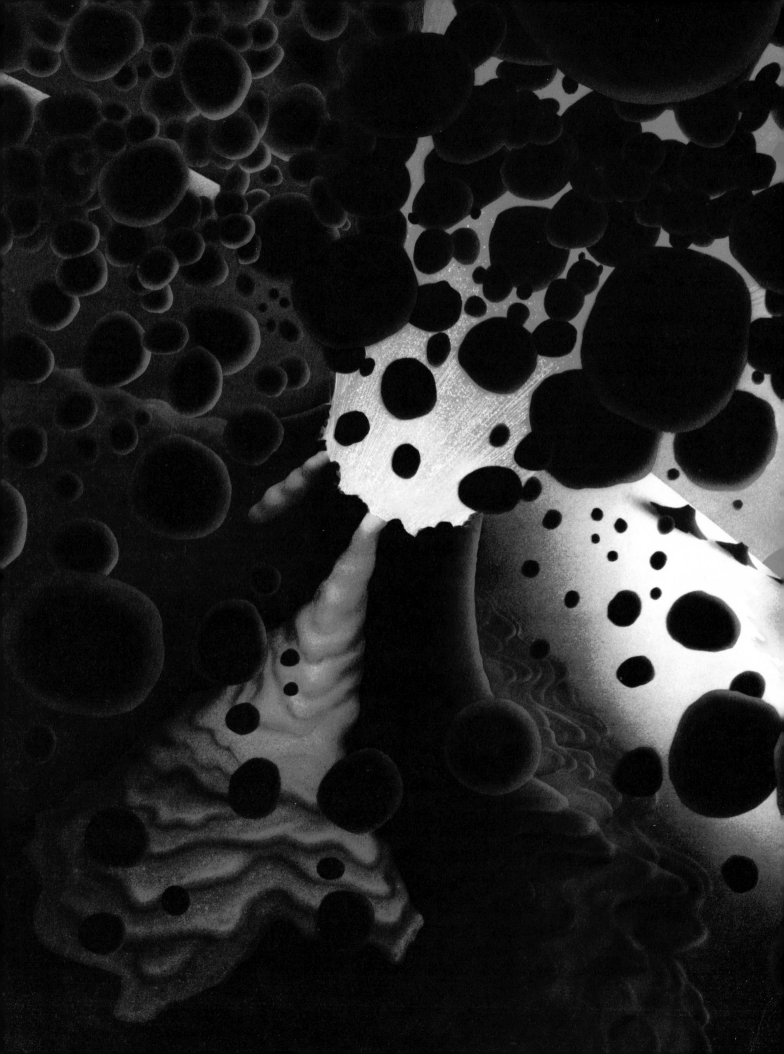

A world without life is far from dead

It is a world in slow turmoil, whose surface is constantly being stirred around, battered, crumpled, eaten away; raised up, folded down, buried . . . in a vast and ceaseless movement of materials and energy. A lively world even before it becomes a living one.

There are the volcanoes, coughing up the Earth's first atmosphere of methane, ammonia, carbon dioxide and steam – and bringing up, too, a rich haul of minerals that would otherwise lie forever locked deep in the depths of the rock. They form new mountains, new layers on the granite rafts and basalt crust of the world. When the steam cools and falls as rain it dissolves a fraction of everything it touches.

The winds in the new atmosphere do their share of destruction, too. They sandblast and scour the bare rock, flaking it, undercutting it, making it crumble. The flakes and grit dissolve in the water. In only a few million years the Earth's gathering lakes, rivers and shallow seas are a thin "soup" – a liquid sample of everything on the surface and in the air above it.

But it is water which utterly changes the character of the Earth. For instance, in the heat at the equator the water turns to vapor. From there it can go only north or south, to cooler regions. There it condenses and falls as rain; but as it does so it gives out the heat it took in when it first vaporized. In other words, the water ferries heat from the equator to the cooler regions. It stabilizes the Earth's temperature and reduces its extremes.

Moreover, the complex air currents inside clouds create huge electric charges, which the water droplets can carry until the burden becomes too great. Then all that electricity discharges in one mighty flash of lightning, the energy of which can force chemicals to combine that would otherwise remain separate to the end of time.

Another thing: water is slower to heat up and takes longer to cool down than many other liquids. So anything in it is protected from sudden and violent temperature changes.

If water did not have these remarkable properties, life could not have begun on Earth.

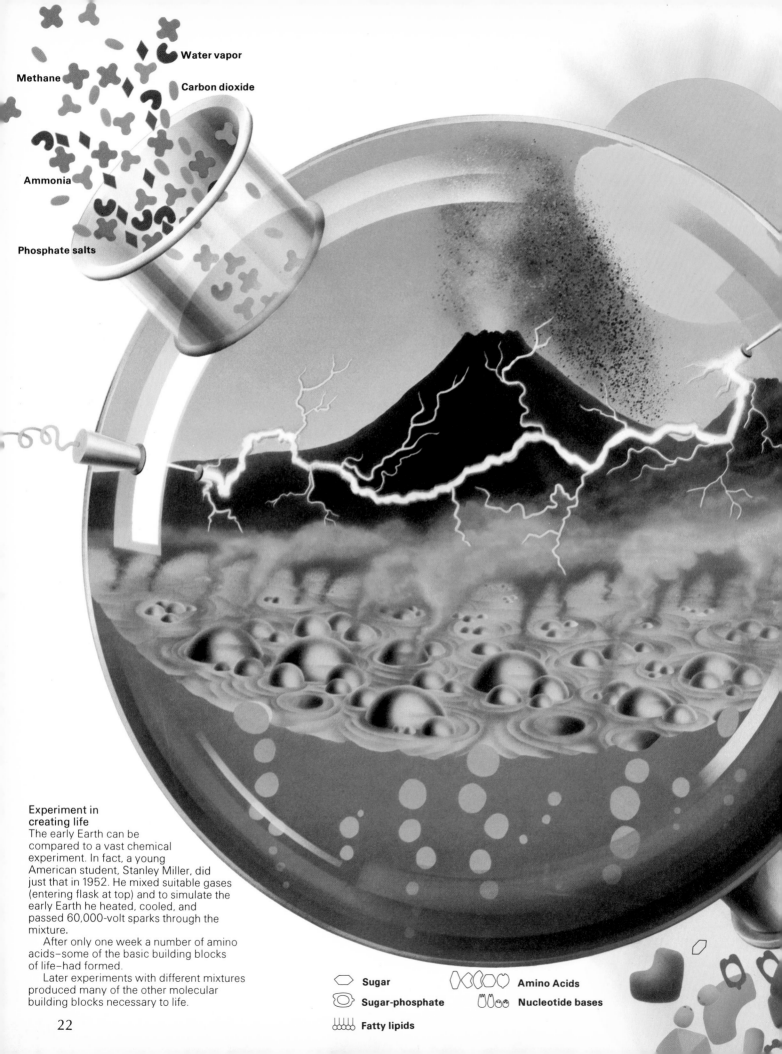

Water vapor

Methane

Carbon dioxide

Ammonia

Phosphate salts

**Experiment in
creating life**
The early Earth can be
compared to a vast chemical
experiment. In fact, a young
American student, Stanley Miller, did
just that in 1952. He mixed suitable gases
(entering flask at top) and to simulate the
early Earth he heated, cooled, and
passed 60,000-volt sparks through the
mixture.
    After only one week a number of amino
acids–some of the basic building blocks
of life–had formed.
    Later experiments with different mixtures
produced many of the other molecular
building blocks necessary to life.

22

$\bigcirc$ **Sugar**

$\bigcirc$ **Sugar-phosphate**

AAAAA **Fatty lipids**

MMMM **Amino Acids**

MMM **Nucleotide bases**

The Earth is one vast chemical factory

Storms rage, lightning flashes, the sun blisters down. It is all energy battering at the early world. The growing oceans of warm water evaporate, forming clouds which drench the land with rain. Rivers flow, carrying minerals to enrich the salty seas. The thin and poisonous atmosphere of water vapor 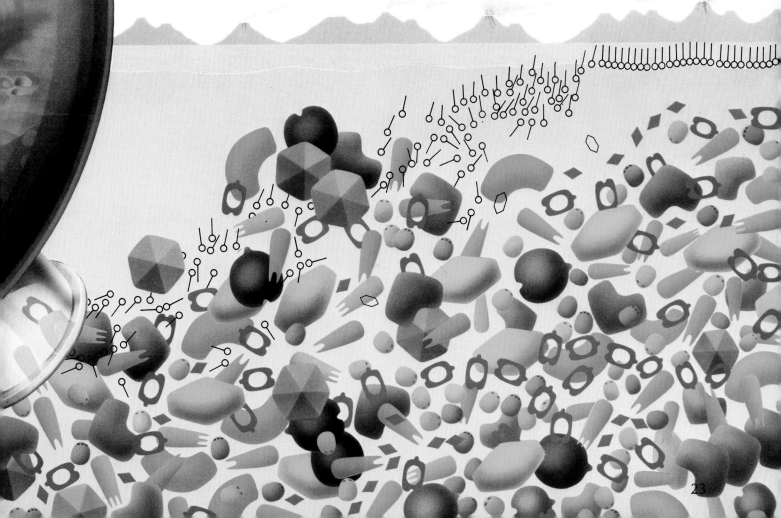, methane, ammonia and carbon dioxide is bombarded by lightning and by radiation. The simple molecules are forced to combine into new larger molecules that are carried down into the sea by the rain.

These new molecules accumulate beneath the surface where they are partly protected from the destructive forces above. Among them are amino acids, fatty lipids, nucleotide bases and mineral salts such as phosphate from the rivers. The phosphates combine with sugars to form sugar-phosphates. These few molecules (and there were many more in the "soup") are the chief characters in the rearrangement that leads to life; an unbelievably slow and random process that will take at least a billion years to accomplish. But the materials are already there. The atoms in those molecules are the same as the atoms in you – every atom in your body is somewhere there in that primitive sea and rock.

If there had been any creature around, it would have called those molecules "food," since the energy that bonded them together could be extracted by breaking the bonds up again. But while there was no such creature, the molecules piled up beneath the surface, packing ever closer together, making an ever richer "soup."

23

An endless two-way traffic…
building up…breaking down

Life could not begin in the early atmosphere because the molecules could never get close enough. Life could not start in the rocks because the molecules were too densely packed to move. Only in the water of the early world could our chief characters wander to and fro, drifting into each other, forming random associations.

Strange chance meetings occur. Those amino acids 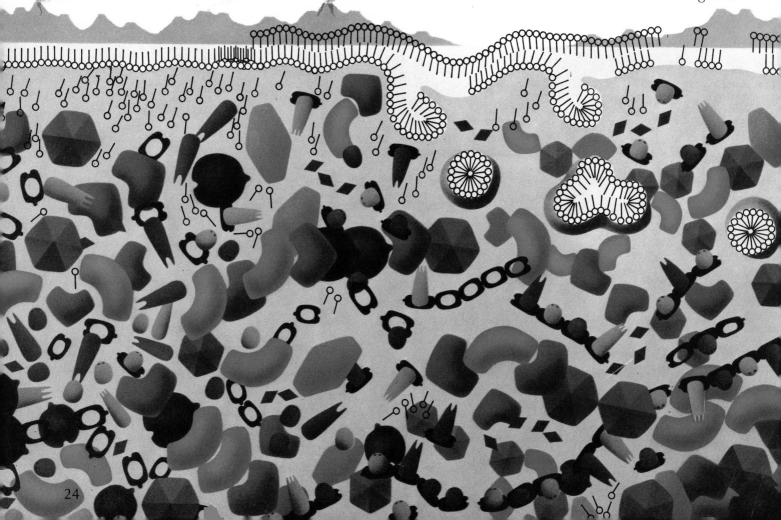 activated by the energy from the atmosphere behave like magnets – so they snap together whenever they get close enough and form long lines , called proteins.

And the sugar-phosphates clip together with any of the four bases ; so we have nucleotides . Some get activated by energy and, drifting randomly, join together to form chains called nucleic acids

Up on the surface of the soup the fatty lipids congregate tail up. One end loves water, the other end hates it. When crowded some may flip over and form a double layer which can sink into the soup.

One day those double layers will form a protective envelope around the lines and chains of amino acids and nucleic acids. But not yet. The whole chemical situation is still too unstable. Because the energy that batters the soup and forces its molecules to combine also batters the combinations and splits them up again.

There's an endless two-way traffic, building up, breaking down. But very very slowly the building up gains on the breaking down.

Time passes, hundreds of millions of years. Non-life goes on. The "food" piles up and associations form … break up … form again … gradually gaining stability and strength.

An important step came when one chain of nucleic acids formed into a double chain. A single

24

The chemicals pile up in the soup
Simple chemicals drift endlessly in the early sea, randomly joining and parting. After many millions of years these begin to form larger molecules in the shape of lines and chains. Small droplets of rain help the fatty lipids to break and form bubbles in the water. The radiation in the atmosphere is so intense that nothing can survive in the harsh environment above the water.

chain is exposed and flimsy. But when each nucleotide 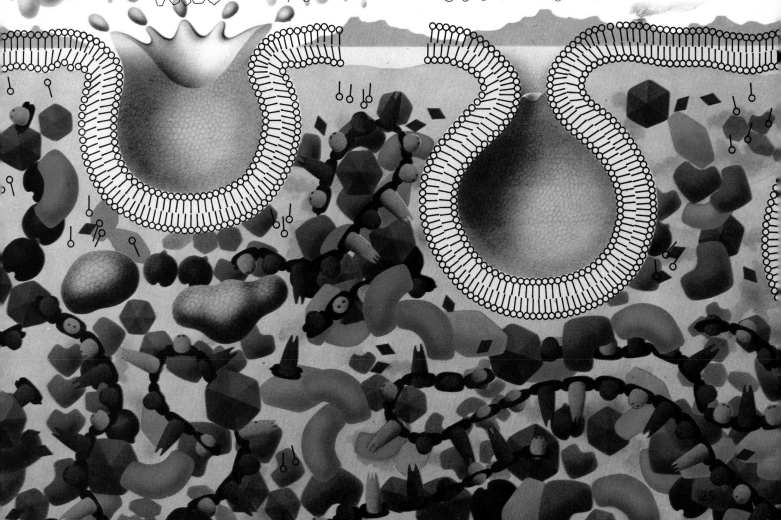 can plug into its own complementary nucleotide the resulting double chain with no exposed plugs and sockets is stronger and more stable. It is called DNA (short for Deoxyribonucleic Acid). And it has the useful ability to unzip and automatically form identical copies of itself from the nucleotides around it.

Another step came when a long line of amino acids joined with another and curled up with it to make a double line or cluster . In these forms they gained a kind of protection and were therefore more stable – not much, but you only have to be a little more stable to be a success.

The great moment comes when one of the lines of amino acids joins up with another of a different type, forming a cluster which is greedier for more amino acids . So they grow more

quickly. It is an enormous advantage to co-operate and help each other to grow in size and variety. This process is self-accelerating because greater variety creates more chances of such mutual help.

But it is still slow, still very random. One is here, and another is way over there. It takes an age for them to drift through the soup. Somehow we have to get them together and keep them there.

And that was the next step. Rain droplets falling on the surface helped to disturb the thin film of fatty lipids causing bits of it to fall below the surface, naturally making little bubbles. Many times they trapped those double chains of nucleic acids and clusters of amino acids It was just the chance they needed. A refuge from all that disorder and chaos outside.

What's more, individual amino acids could penetrate the membrane – and so could the bases and sugars

Chaos . . . order . . . stability . . . life

Safe within their bubbles, the lines and chains could now grow in relative peace and quiet. In a world of chemical chaos, tiny pockets of order began to appear. Protection is so important to life that nature has continued to use membranes (or skin, or bark, or scales, or some kind of barrier against chaos) ever since.

Shielded from the chaos, the lines and chains prospered and grew more stable; so much so that they quickly outgrew their membranes. Whenever that happened, the membrane burst and re-formed into smaller bubbles, each with a part of the original contents. A primitive kind of reproduction had been achieved, but in that early soup it was an uncontrolled and chancy event.

How to make it less chancy – that was the next problem. The answer was closely tied in with the answer to another problem – "death." Those curled up lines of amino acids 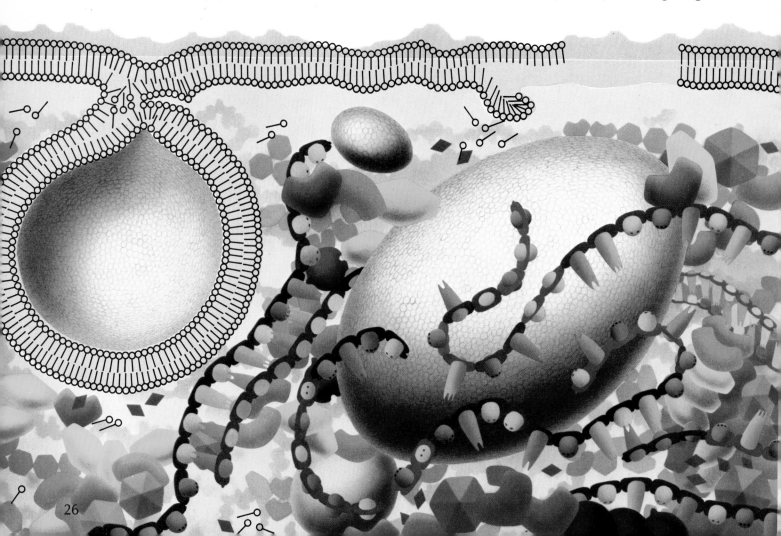, or proteins, weren't lasting forever. Even in their new, relatively stable situation they would break down. How to replace them? Somehow a way had to be found to record the exact sequence of amino acids in a given protein so that copies could be made. What was around in the soup that could help?

How about those nucleic acid chains – DNA? Their four bases make a perfect code for recording which amino acids link up and in what order. The code works in triplets. For instance, specifies amino acid , but specifies amino acid , and specifies amino acid . . . and so on.

So if you put all nine bases together in that particular order, you will find those three amino acids – *and no others* – lining up alongside, like boats docking at their own particular jetty. The amazing thing is

Bubbles form skins for the first cells
Fatty lipid bubbles begin to enclose stable chemicals in the soup and protect them from the chaos outside. These will become the first cells. On reaching a certain size, the bubbles will break into smaller bubbles – the first kind of reproduction. To the right is a primitive cell, cut away to show the inside. Single amino acids drift in through the wall and add to the protein inside. DNA can be seen specifying the order of amino acids to make protein. Nucleotides are forming new DNA chains. Compared to the workings of today's cells these processes were inefficient and random.

that as soon as they are docked they link up bow to stern and peel off from the nucleic acid chain, which is then free to attract another three identical amino acids . . . then another . . . and another.

Imagine a chain with hundreds of bases and you have a perfect little factory for making protein after protein. At last we have the ingredients for a living cell. It has a protective outer membrane. It has DNA, which can make all the proteins the cell needs, and which can duplicate itself.

So the cell can divide into two cells, both viable, whenever conditions are favorable. The earliest versions of the system were probably very crude and imperfect – a far remove from the one used by living things today (where many other molecules are involved).

The cells that gave rise to all living things must have made a further breakthrough to protect their DNA from undue wear and tear. DNA became a master copy of the specification for every protein in the cell. To make protein it unzips itself and makes a copy of one of its halves. That copy (called RNA, Ribonucleic Acid) goes out and does all the rough and tumble work of joining up the amino acids – again and again and again. If it gets damaged, the DNA can simply unzip once again and run off another strand of RNA to go out and replace the damaged molecule.

Another great advance toward stability came when some proteins began to act as accelerators of these processes while others took on the role of brakes. Now the primitive little cell could surge forward when food energy was abundant and go very steady when the supply fell off. It could begin to *respond* to its environment.

It could begin to live.

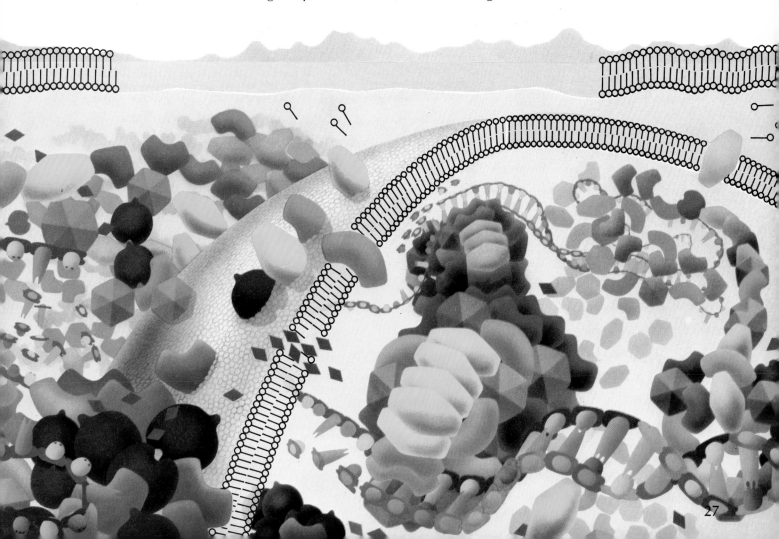

27

Self-sufficiency . . . breaking the food barrier

The violent energy that helped to create life could also rip it apart, killing the primitive cells that got too close to the surface of the sea. Mistakes in copying the DNA could also have taken their toll.

These dead cells offered a new lease of life to any cell that could find a way of breaking them down and plundering their chemical treasures. That way had to be by making new kinds of proteins – digestive proteins which would break open the membrane, and break down the proteins, sugars and other molecules into smaller bits that could be absorbed and reassembled to allow growth.

How do you make a new kind of protein? The only way is to change the message on the DNA – put a 🐸 for a 🐸 or a 🐽 for a 🐸 – get it to specify something different. How? Only chance can do that. Radiation damage, a copying error, an accidental joining up in the DNA, chemical damage

– these can change DNA, and once a change is established, the DNA will go on making changed copies until the next mistake. We call such a change a "mutation."

The marvelous thing about this system is that it *automatically* promotes improvements. For if a mutation is harmful, the cell dies – and the DNA dies with it. But beneficial mutations help the cell to survive and multiply.

Almost all mutations are harmful; only a one-in-a-thousand lucky chance is beneficial. Nevertheless the whole of evolution has gone forward powered by this one process. It was such mutations, way back at the beginning, that eventually produced digestive proteins. The first primitive cells that developed such proteins and could ransack the dead cells of their chemical treasures were "scavengers." Today we call them bacteria.

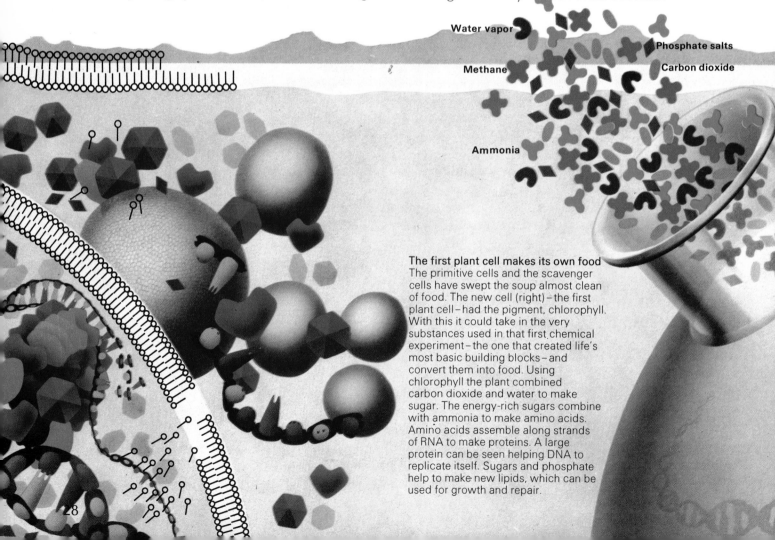

Water vapor

Phosphate salts

Methane Carbon dioxide

Ammonia

The first plant cell makes its own food
The primitive cells and the scavenger cells have swept the soup almost clean of food. The new cell (right) – the first plant cell – had the pigment, chlorophyll. With this it could take in the very substances used in that first chemical experiment – the one that created life's most basic building blocks – and convert them into food. Using chlorophyll the plant combined carbon dioxide and water to make sugar. The energy-rich sugars combine with ammonia to make amino acids. Amino acids assemble along strands of RNA to make proteins. A large protein can be seen helping DNA to replicate itself. Sugars and phosphate help to make new lipids, which can be used for growth and repair.

28

There was one great barrier that life still had to break: the food barrier. All the primitive cells depended for food on the random formation of molecules by heat, radiation, lightning and other forms of energy. It was steady – but oh so slow.

Soon the food was getting snapped up as quickly as it was made. If only the cells could *make* food for themselves. To do that they needed energy from outside. But it had to be a mild form of energy, so that it wouldn't damage the DNA and disrupt the cell's chemistry.

There is only one regular, worldwide source of such energy: the sun. Even when the sky is overcast, daylight still filters through. What the cell needed was a means of trapping that daylight energy. Answer: a pigment. The building blocks for pigments were already there in the soup.

The first cells probably made pigments to protect themselves from the sun's harmful ultraviolet radiation, just as the pigment does in our skin today. When daylight hits most pigments it turns to heat. But it would just need a different series of mutations to make chlorophyll, the green pigment in plants.

Chlorophyll is special. It turns a small part of daylight into electricity – a much more useful form of energy. With its help the cell takes molecules of carbon dioxide and water to build molecules of sugar which is rich in energy. The byproduct of the process is oxygen, which is a poison to anything that grew up in a methane-ammonia atmosphere. Even so, the advantage of being able to make your own food was so great that cells learned to tolerate the poison oxygen rather than give up and go back to the old system. Soon the oceans blushed green with a new form of life – plant cells.

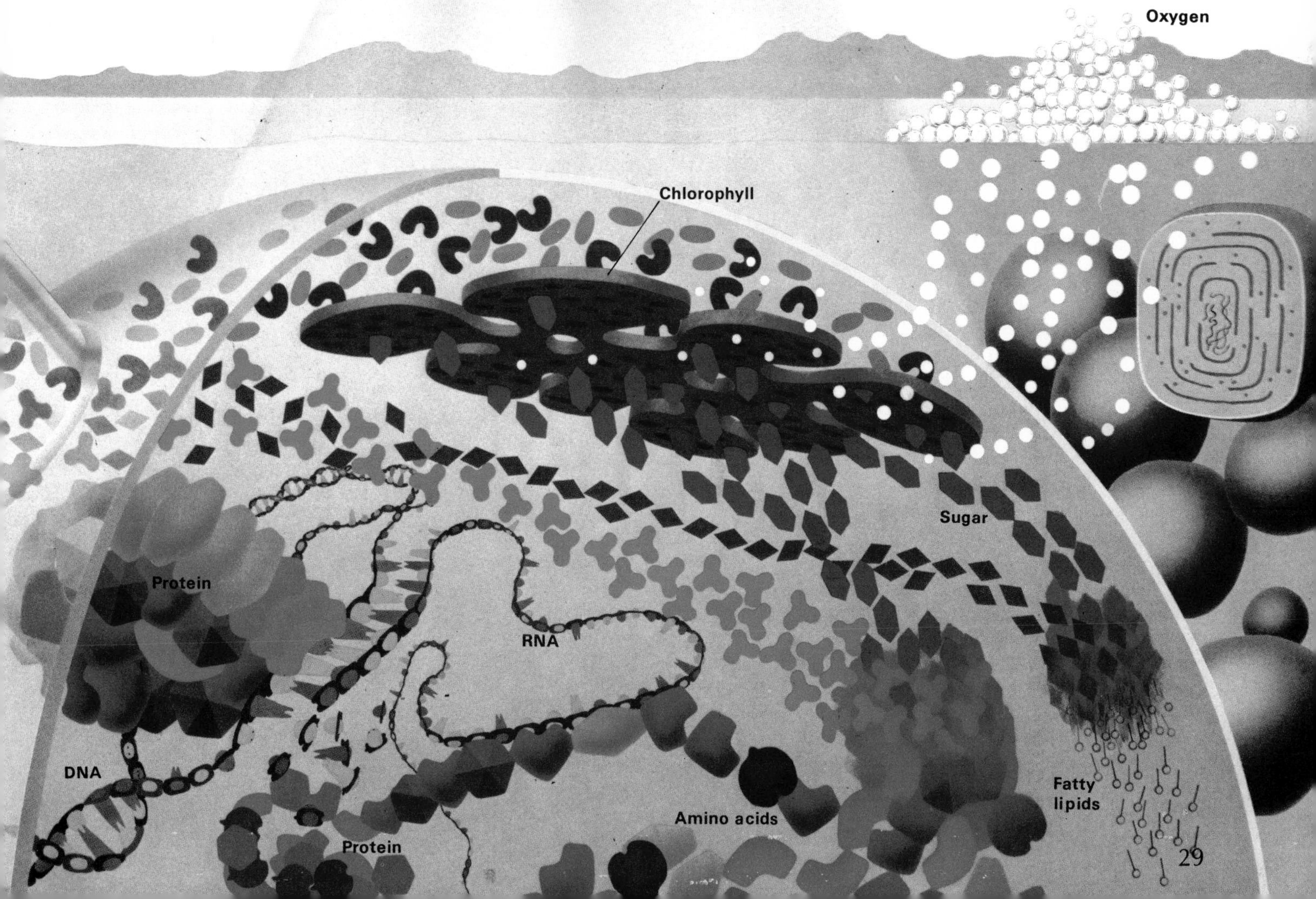

Oxygen

Chlorophyll

Sugar

Protein

RNA

DNA

Fatty lipids

Amino acids

Protein

29

Everything in that early soup is now in you

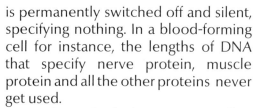

Two-and-a-half billion years have passed since the formation of the Earth, and we are already half way to the present. It has taken all that time to create the first plant – and that plant has just one cell.

Now, look at the cells on the page opposite. There are 50 trillion like them at work in your body right this instant – sense cells of the inner ear, blood cells, muscle, nerve, skin, liver cells … they are only a fraction of the many different kinds of cells that make up you. What makes them different is, chiefly, their proteins: hemoglobin in the blood, actin and myosin in muscle, keratin in skin cells . . . and so on. It is the shape and the chemical personality of these proteins which is vital to you.

And the remarkable thing is that the proteins in all your trillions of cells are specified by the same process as the proteins in that very first cell billions of years ago. DNA, the code which carried the message then, is still hard at it. Only the message on it has changed over time, to specify plants, animals and man. But how much DNA does it take to specify all the proteins in a human being?

You already know the basic system. A typical protein consists of, let's say, two hundred amino acids joined together. Each amino acid is specified by a sequence of three units in the DNA chain: ⌣⌣⌣ for instance, or ⌣⌣⌣ . So to make just one of your proteins calls for something like 600 of those units.

And, in fact, human DNA has about three-and-a-half billion units. Stretched end to end they would reach about two yards – not bad when you remember that a typical cell is only five millionths of a yard across. If the DNA in all 50 trillion of the cells in your body were laid end to end they would stretch 62 billion miles.

And every cell has *all* the DNA necessary to specify an entire person. So most of it, in most cells, is permanently switched off and silent, specifying nothing. In a blood-forming cell for instance, the lengths of DNA that specify nerve protein, muscle protein and all the other proteins never get used.

But don't think that once a cell is formed, all it has to do is to carry out its function until you die. Individual cells in tissues all over your body are dying all the time; all of them, except your nerve cells, can repair the loss by new growth. Scratch your skin and you kill millions of cells, but all the dead ones will be removed and replaced within days. Every second two to three million of your red blood cells die and are replaced. These are dismantled by your liver (which uses some of the products to make bile salts to aid digestion). Taste bud cells last only five days on average – in fact, all the cells that come into physical contact with the outside world undergo incredibly rapid turnover.

Different cells regenerate in different ways. A liver cell, for instance, dies and shrivels, so its neighbor divides in two and makes up the number again. When it divides, its DNA duplicates by unzipping completely, then each half regenerates its missing partner. While the two new cells are developing, the DNA which specifies their proteins stays temporarily active until they are full-size. Finally only the bits of DNA that specify that cell's particular function in your body stay active.

Some parts of the DNA act as regulators – starting, stopping, hastening, or slowing down the activity of other parts of the DNA. For instance, you get a minor infection, your white blood cells fight the invader, and some die and break down. The breakdown products stimulate the DNA in other white cells to switch on a massive multiplication strategy and soon millions of white cells stand off the invader.

But to understand how this extraordinary complexity of cells evolved from that first plant cell we must return to the early sea.

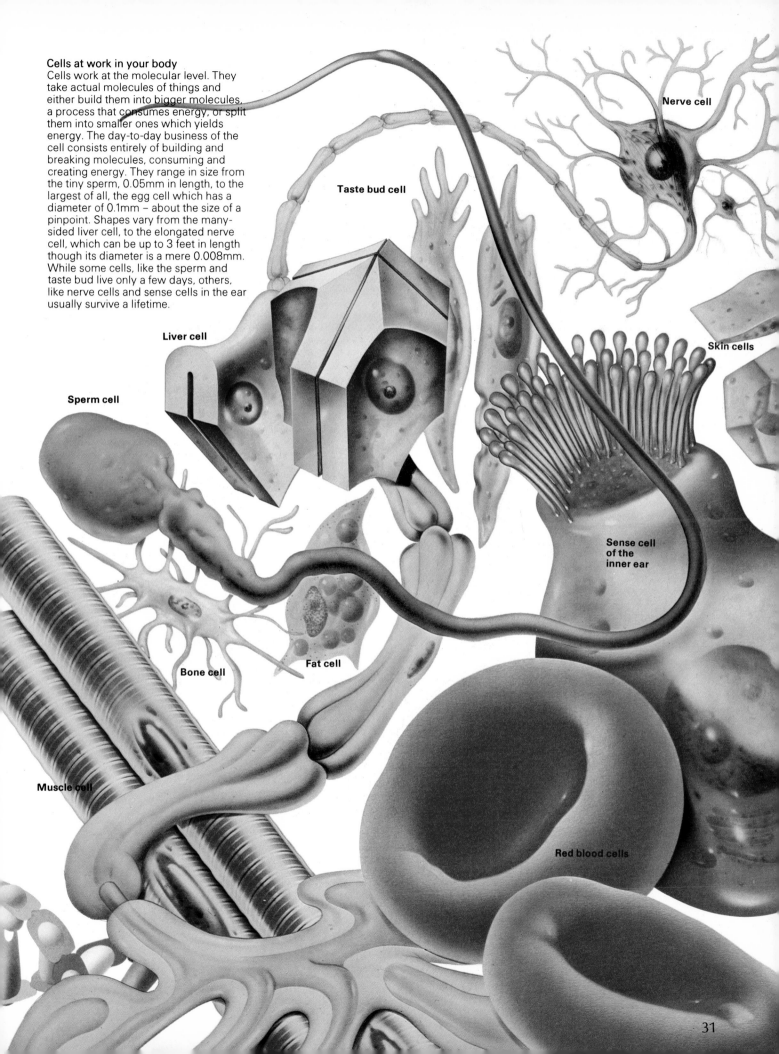

Cells at work in your body

Cells work at the molecular level. They take actual molecules of things and either build them into bigger molecules, a process that consumes energy, or split them into smaller ones which yields energy. The day-to-day business of the cell consists entirely of building and breaking molecules, consuming and creating energy. They range in size from the tiny sperm, 0.05mm in length, to the largest of all, the egg cell which has a diameter of 0.1mm – about the size of a pinpoint. Shapes vary from the many-sided liver cell, to the elongated nerve cell, which can be up to 3 feet in length though its diameter is a mere 0.008mm. While some cells, like the sperm and taste bud live only a few days, others, like nerve cells and sense cells in the ear usually survive a lifetime.

Taste bud cell

Nerve cell

Liver cell

Skin cells

Sperm cell

Sense cell of the inner ear

Bone cell

Fat cell

Muscle cell

Red blood cells

31

When success threatened survival

Developing in that early sea was a simple community of mutually dependent living creatures. Countless millions of tiny plant cells floated near the surface, using chlorophyll to convert the sun's energy into the food that they needed to grow and multiply.

Almost as fast as they multiplied, others died from the effects of radiation and sank to the seabed. There they formed an abundant source of food for scavenger cells, which broke them down by sending out digestive proteins and absorbed the chemical treasures through their cell walls. But it was a hit-or-miss affair, sitting still waiting for the dead cells to drift down within reach. Sooner or later a more efficient method of acquiring and absorbing food had to evolve.

The cells that first developed the ability to surround a dead cell and absorb its riches without wasting their own digestive proteins were the new champions. To do this, they had to grow larger in size; a little further mutation and they had gained the power of simple movement, which meant that the abundant source of food on the surface was there for the taking – the living plant cells. These newly-evolved cells were, by definition, the first animals, for an animal is a creature that lives by eating plants (or by eating other animals that eat plants). And they had the choice of feeding on the plant cells above, the scavenger cells below or the dead cells drifting in between. You would think they must have scooped the pool.

Not so. The system was balanced because there could only be as many animal cells and scavenger cells as could be supported by the plant cells. The same thing is true of every living community we know today.

Plants nourish animals; but animals destroy plants. It's a very stable pattern. However much you disturb it, it tends to settle back into equilibrium. Suppose that, for some reason, there is a sudden abundance of plant food, animals multiply, as they always do in good times. More plants get devoured and the abundance vanishes. Now there's a lot of starving animals. Many perish and the survivors don't breed so prolifically. The plants,

no longer over-cropped, recover. The animals recover, too.

This point is vitally important to all living things in our own era. Certainly it is true that today, about two billion years after plants and animals first evolved, their ways of life are so inextricably interwoven it would be hard to show that the advantages and disadvantages of either did not more or less balance.

Take the case of grass. On the east African plain is one of the world's last great grassland wildernesses, where antelope, wildebeest, and zebra graze. When you see these herds all mixed up together, you'd think they were all competing for the same food. Not a bit of it. The three eat entirely different grasses, different lengths, different textures. What is more, their grazing helps keep down the sort of scrub plants that would soon invade the place and smother the grasses. And if the tall, coarse grasses beloved of the zebra were not grazed, the finer, succulent grasses the wildebeest favor would not flourish. So their interdependence is total – grasses and animals.

As animals and plants evolved into an ever-increasing variety of forms, so their communities became more complex and more stable. But the relationships remained the same. Plants trap the sun's energy and make food, giving out the surplus oxygen. Animals eat the plants, or eat animals that eat plants. The animals' wastes, their dung and urine and their bodies when they die and dead plants, too, are food for creatures such as insects, bacteria and fungi. Ultimately it is all broken down again into simple chemicals out of which a new generation of plants grows. A perfect cycle, kept turning by the sun's energy.

Of course, in order to keep this system in balance, the plants and animals have to solve their individual problems of survival in the first place. Back in that primitive sea, they had encountered another obstacle. Poison. As those first plant cells thrived so they produced more and more oxygen. Remember that Earth had never produced free oxygen – the gas. Earth's oxygen had always been safely combined with other atoms: CO_2 for instance, and H$_2$O, and numerous kinds of crystal and mineral. But free, gaseous oxygen was a corrosive, poisonous gas, lethal to all forms of life that had grown up in a methane and ammonia atmosphere. So their very success seemed to threaten their survival. In the event they turned this problem to great advantage.

If you are a cell and you get given a sugar molecule there are two ways of getting energy out of it. The primitive way is to ferment it to alcohol, and until oxygen came along, that was the only way.

But oxygen allows you to burn the sugar. Not with flames, but the end result is the same – the sugar is broken back into carbon dioxide and water, the very substances from which the plant cell builds up the sugar in the first place. The amazing thing is that the oxygen way produces 19 times more energy than the fermentation way.

The first cell to achieve the mutation that put oxygen to work on sugars was a plant cell. And it gained a phenomenal advantage, for it required only one-nineteenth of the food intake that a cell dependent on fermentation required.

Animal cells at the surface made the same break-through independently, but very little oxygen reached the scavengers on the ocean floor and we find that their descendants, yeasts and some bacteria, still use the primitive way of breaking sugar without oxygen.

All cells in all other living things use the oxygen route to energy – except when oxygen is scarce, as in our bodies when we run fast and need energy faster than the oxygen can be supplied to our muscles. In such emergencies we use the fermentation way of breaking sugar until we can relax and give the oxygen a chance to burn the sugar all the way to carbon dioxide and water.

The buildup of oxygen in the atmosphere was having other effects. It filtered out most of the sun's deadly radiation, a change that would one day enable life to colonize the land. Even today, if we were to lose that precious filter in the atmosphere, all life on land might perish. But that same radiation had been supplying the "soup" with amino acids for hundreds of millions of years and that supply was already dwindling as more and more plant cells used them up. The animal and scavenger cells were affected only indirectly because they get their amino acids by eating plant cells.

The plant cells solved this problem with more mutations in their DNA which enabled them to make all their amino acids from their store of sugar. Since then, all plants have been completely self-sufficient, provided that they have mineral salts in their water supply.

But we humans can make only about half the amino acids we need. The rest we have to get from our food.

The oxygen way of life opened up another source of food for some special scavenger cells. With the help of oxygen they could take in that ammonia and methane still in the atmosphere, digest and convert it into nitrogen, water and carbon dioxide.

Nitrogen? Water? Carbon dioxide? The world is suddenly becoming a very familiar place.

These two sets of mutations, the one for chlorophyll and the one for oxygen burning, became the basis for an entirely new way of life.

With chlorophyll the amount of food that the whole world had been producing could now be created in a few square miles of ocean. And oxygen made it possible to use those foodstuffs 19 times more effectively than before.

The sheer weight of living matter which the Earth could now support must have multiplied hundreds of millions of times over. Naturally, the quantity of DNA in the world multiplied by a similar amount. The workshop in which mutations could occur was now vast. Life was already more than half-way down its evolutionary path, but now it was poised to make some really spectacular advances – once it had consolidated its newly won position.

Safety in numbers . . . the beginning of specialization

Four billion years have now passed – four-fifths of the Earth's history to the present day. The single-celled way of life has spread a long way through the seas, into shallow inlets, lagoons and mudflats. More DNA – more chances of mutations.

Being single-celled has its disadvantages. For instance, you have to live in water. So, being forced to stay in the water, you are highly vulnerable to drought. Also you can't move very fast or very far to escape being eaten by other cells.

There are two ways of insuring against these risks. One is the safety-in-numbers policy. Successful single-celled creatures can band together into simple colonies where each individual cell gains protection but still has to perform all the functions such as feeding, growth and reproduction.

The other answer is for us a major evolutionary breakthrough, the division of labor between cells – a multicellular organism. Although the DNA is the same in all the cells of a multicellular organism, certain parts switch off so that cells have different functions such as food gathering, food transporting, and skeleton making.

The first multicellular creatures were like the modern Obelia (illustrated), built like a sack, with waving tentacles around its mouth out of which it can also empty the indigestible bits and other waste products.

The sack body plan has its limitations. Feeding is a batch process rather than the assembly-line – in one end, out the other – type of digestive system. All the cells have to stay really close to the great lagoon of the sackgut; otherwise they starve. That, in turn, limits the size and the degree of complexity.

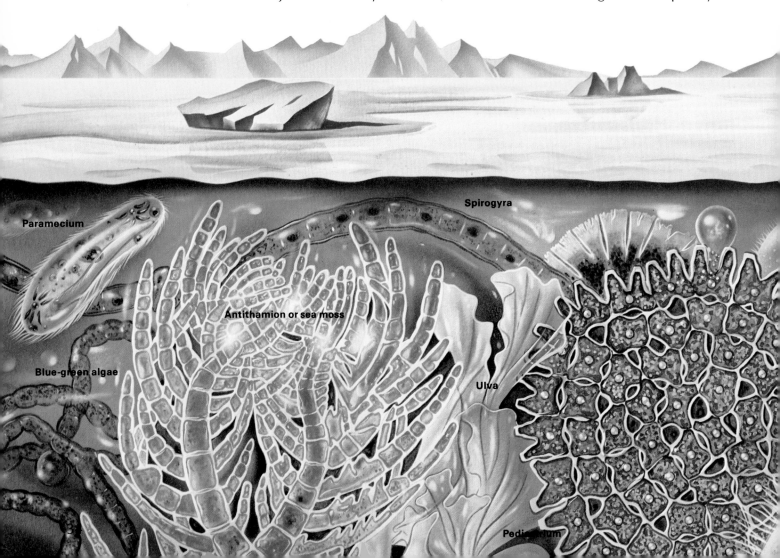

Paramecium

Spirogyra

Antithamion or sea moss

Blue-green algae

Ulva

Pediastrum

With only two layers to the body there is little scope for muscular movement, so they tend to be rooted to the bottom of the pool or free-floating like the jellyfish.

A more promising arrangement was the tube gut with two openings to allow continuous feeding. All creatures built around a tube gut have three basic body layers. An inner one to process food; an outer one to gather data from the world and to protect against it; and a middle layer in which a cavity can form so as to allow movements of the gut and the animal to be independent of each other.

This arrangement allowed a great increase in body size and opened up great new possibilities; virtually all multicelled creatures are now organized on this body plan. In the middle layer has evolved a blood system to distribute the oxygen and digested food to outlying cells. A central nervous system led to faster coordination of movement, and muscle attached to skeletons could move the body very much more effectively.

And being multicellular had a disadvantage that became an advantage in the long run. Single-celled creatures can reproduce by dividing, creating huge populations of carbon copies – strength in numbers but not in diversity. But because a multicellular organism had specialized cells it was no more able to divide than we are.

Instead special sex cells had to join to produce offspring. The mingling of their two DNAs created both good and poor organisms, of which the more adaptive survived while the rest died out. This was the first sexual reproduction and it gave an enormous boost to change and to evolution.

Volvox

Vorticella

Obelia

35

Many separate laboratories

Things happen on Earth that are totally unaffected by the presence of life. They would go on happening if every living thing vanished overnight – and they were happening long before life began.

Stand on any seashore and look out over the ocean. Think of the land underfoot, running down below the waves to the ocean bed and then rising somewhere else, through another fringe of waves to another shore, another land. Nothing, you might think, could be more solid than that. Yet, those solid-seeming continents are floating in the rock of the earth's mantle, which flows like ice in a glacier.

Some 650 million years ago, about the time that animal life began to diversify, a number of granite rafts, in no way shaped like our present continents, began a long crashing together that took about 200 million years to complete. The result was one supercontinent – now known as Pangea.

At that time, 440 million years ago, when the supercontinent formed, all animal life, and most plant life, too, was still confined to the sea and lakes and rivers. But by the time Pangea began to split up again, 300 million years later, life had spread to every part of the land. The great age of the dinosaurs was at its height, but the mammals and birds, and the flowering plants, grasses, and trees were not yet fully established.

Antarctica-India and Australia were first to go 140 million years ago; then South America 20 million years later – and at the same time India peeled off from Antarctica and began to migrate towards Asia; North America split from Europe-Asia only 65 million years ago; and finally India rammed into Asia 30 million years ago, piling up the huge Himalayan ranges.

Breakups like these, and the barriers formed by new mountain ranges and sea, acted as a further spur to evolution. They created, in effect, many separate laboratories in which DNA would come up with different answers to similar problems. But it is surprising how alike many of those different answers turned out to be.

For instance, among the mammals there were two main evolutionary lines: the familiar placentals that include ourselves, and the marsupials that give birth to very immature young, which complete their development in the safety of their mothers' fur or pouch. The first mammals on Pangea were the marsupials, and these survived on the early breakaway continents of South America and Australia. Elsewhere the more efficient placental mammals displaced the marsupials.

Nonetheless Australia has a marsupial version of the wolf and there are marsupial mice and rats as well. All have evolved in response to environments similar to those of their placental counterparts, though they have utterly different ancestry. An exception is the kangaroo – the placental equivalent of which was the horse.

Not only did the breakup of Pangea let evolution take different paths in isolation; but the movement of these new continents promoted great climatic changes. These would have ended a favored way of life for some plants and animals, but opened up new opportunities for others. In this way DNA was constantly, although slowly, experiencing new conditions that allowed different mutations a chance of success. The result is the huge diversity of life on Earth today.

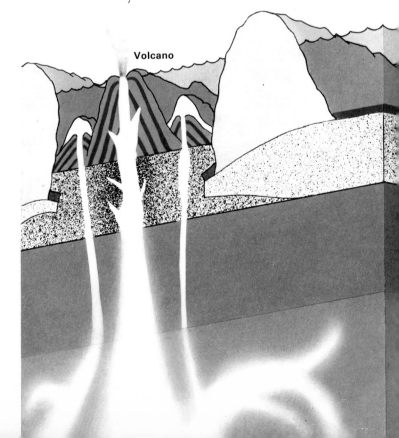

Volcano

The moving continents
The outer core of the Earth is molten rock. Above this lies a thick layer of dense, solid rock, the mantle. The crust forms a thin, outer skin extending beneath both oceans and continents. Land masses are formed where a second layer of rock sits on top of the crust. The crust consists of a number of separate plates. In moving continuously over the mantle, neighboring plates collide, or split apart to leave gaps in the crust. Where collision occurs, mountain folds may be thrown up. Where gaps form, molten rock from the core forces its way up, creating volcanoes.

Asia

India

140 million years ago
above
There was a single land mass that we call Pangea. Pressures within the underlying crust were starting to pull it apart.

India

Asia

65 million years ago
above
Pangea had split into two – Laurasia in the north and Gondwanaland in the south. The latter then broke up into the South American, African, Indian and combined Antarctican-Australian plates

Himalayas

Sea level

Ocean

India

Asia

Crust

Present day
above
The Indian plate has collided with the Eurasian, thrusting up the Himalayas, while the Australian and Antarctican plates have separated. The North and South American have united, and the African plate has joined to the Eurasian plate.

Mantle

37

They crawled onto the land and brought the sea with them

By 440 million years ago, when the world's one ocean was lapping the shores of an almost barren Pangea, the creatures built on the tube principle had made amazing progress.

One group had arrived at the fish – with a head, eyes and other sense organs, a muscular tail, flexible spine and steering fins, all controlled by a central nervous system. Such a system allowed faster and more coordinated movement. Faster predators promote faster prey – a case of evolutionary escalation that rapidly perfects a particular body form.

The fish also had a heart with pumping chambers and a gut with specialized compartments for the different stages of digesting food. It had kidneys to filter wastes from the blood; a liver to handle most of the body chemistry; and male or female sex organs where the DNA of the next generation was stored.

The really extraordinary thing is that most of the vertebrate evolutionary developments since then have been mere variations of that basic fish plan. Every organ in that list has its exact counterpart in you and me. The bones of the fish fin, for instance, can be traced through numerous forms to the bones of your arms and legs. Most of the fish's organs even bear the same name as their human counterparts. Once life has come up with a successful plan, it adapts and adapts that plan to ever-changing circumstances – rarely does it scrap a design and begin all over. Even when life took to the land, it did so with an adapted fish body.

It's hard for us to realize what a great step it was for creatures to move out onto the land. In fact, they did so only by bringing the sea with them. Even to this day our body is bathed internally in a watery fluid much like that early sea. The amphibians, the first creatures to take that step, were under constant

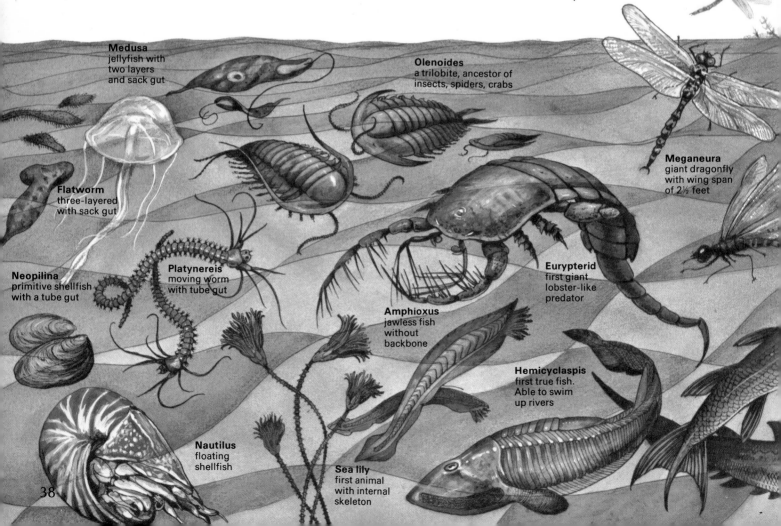

Medusa
jellyfish with two layers and sack gut

Olenoides
a trilobite, ancestor of insects, spiders, crabs

Meganeura
giant dragonfly with wing span of 2½ feet

Flatworm
three-layered with sack gut

Neopilina
primitive shellfish with a tube gut

Platynereis
moving worm with tube gut

Eurypterid
first giant lobster-like predator

Amphioxus
jawless fish without backbone

Hemicyclaspis
first true fish. Able to swim up rivers

Nautilus
floating shellfish

Sea lily
first animal with internal skeleton

Plants were first to colonize the land
Around the shores of Pangea the shallow lagoons and mud flats were constantly drying out. Only cells with tough protective coats could survive. Often such cells were blown inland to freshwater lakes and swamps. There they evolved into colonial and then multicelled forms – liverworts, mosses and ferns. Hot, humid jungles grew up, offering a rich variety of food and shelter for the first insects and amphibians.

threat of drying out. They had simple lungs to obtain oxygen and lose carbon dioxide, and perhaps breathed partly through their damp skin. Most of them were as much at home in the water as on the land – and they all returned to the water to mate.

Nevertheless, for those who made the vital change from water breathing to air breathing, the reward was immense. In time, better lungs would free the skin from its role in breathing and allow it to grow tough and thick – a stout shield against the dangers of drying out. Then there would be a whole, new, uncrowded world to inherit, a world colonized by plants that had no defenses against animals. Riches indeed!

Seymouria
the earliest reptile

Eryops
amphibian ancestor of the reptiles

Hylonomus
possible ancestor of the dinosaurs

Eusthenopteron
early air-breathing fish, a probable ancestor of the amphibians

Ichthyostegalian
the first amphibian

Climatius
fresh water fish with heavy protective scales

39

Lords of the world for a hundred million years

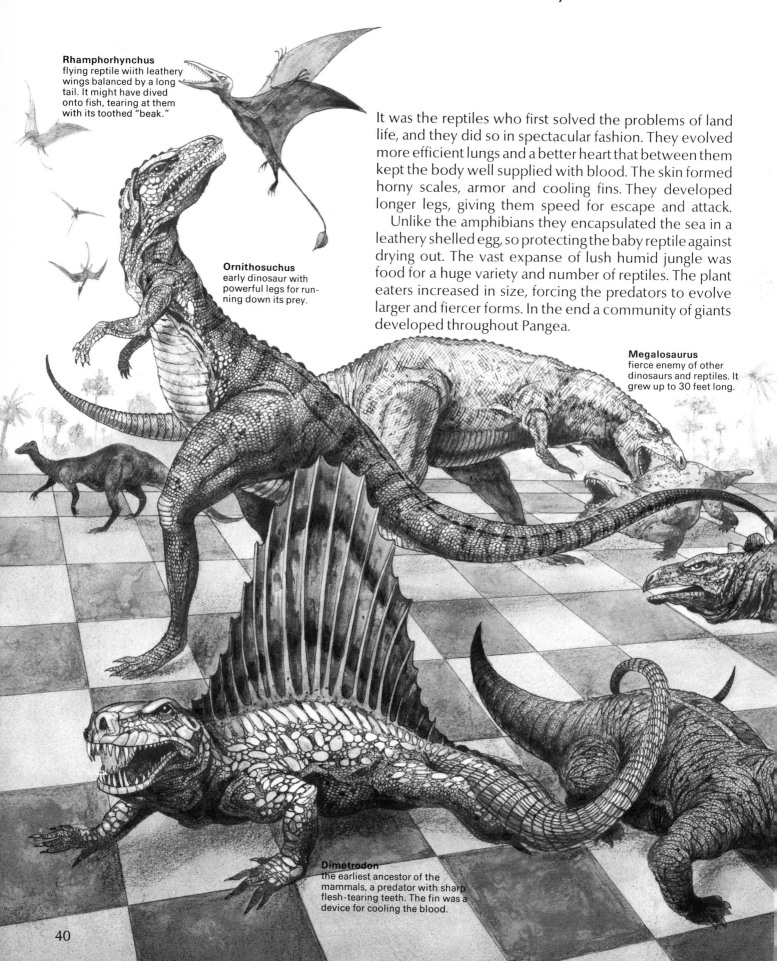

Rhamphorhynchus
flying reptile wiith leathery wings balanced by a long tail. It might have dived onto fish, tearing at them with its toothed "beak."

Ornithosuchus
early dinosaur with powerful legs for running down its prey.

It was the reptiles who first solved the problems of land life, and they did so in spectacular fashion. They evolved more efficient lungs and a better heart that between them kept the body well supplied with blood. The skin formed horny scales, armor and cooling fins. They developed longer legs, giving them speed for escape and attack.

Unlike the amphibians they encapsulated the sea in a leathery shelled egg, so protecting the baby reptile against drying out. The vast expanse of lush humid jungle was food for a huge variety and number of reptiles. The plant eaters increased in size, forcing the predators to evolve larger and fiercer forms. In the end a community of giants developed throughout Pangea.

Megalosaurus
fierce enemy of other dinosaurs and reptiles. It grew up to 30 feet long.

Dimetrodon
the earliest ancestor of the mammals, a predator with sharp flesh-tearing teeth. The fin was a device for cooling the blood.

Reptiles have to keep warm
For most of their reign the dinosaurs lived in a tropical belt rich in vegetation. On a hot day they could be very frisky, but if the temperature dropped they soon grew sluggish. The speed of chemical reactions, including the chemistry of living organisms, depends absolutely on temperature. A reptile with a large body or one that lived partly in water would conserve its body heat and be able to live in more temperate regions.

Archaeopteryx
earliest ancestor of the birds with feathers that evolved from scales. With clawed wings it climbed and then glided down in search of food.

Stegosaurus
large plant-eating dinosaur protected from attack by a double row of armored plates. The spikes on its powerful tail were probably its only other defense.

Morganucodon
one of the earliest mammals, small, agile and feeding on insects. Its hairy coat helped maintain a steady temperature.

Dicynodon
descended from Dimetrodon. This plant-eating reptile had teeth better adapted for its specialized diet and warm blood like its descendants the mammals.

41

The meek inherit the Earth

We often use the dinosaurs as symbols of failure; yet man will have to survive another 125 million years even to equal their record. Exactly why these highly developed reptiles vanished is still something of a mystery.

Because the dinosaurs are all extinct now and their place has been taken by the mammals and birds, we tend to think that these evolved after the dinosaurs. But that isn't so. In fact, the forerunner of the mammals – a little creature that looked something like a rat – was alive not long after the first of the dinosaurs came along.

But the reptiles had already taken up all the options the world had to offer; so there was no way the early mammal could get well established. Meanwhile, the reptiles went on and on specializing – growing bigger, more extreme and (to our eyes) more grotesque in form, culminating in the extraordinary figures of the tyrannosaurs and horned dinosaurs.

But the reptiles had two big disadvantages that were bound to weigh against them in time. They had a poor brain and they couldn't control their body temperature. A good brain needs a highly developed blood supply and a constant temperature. Creatures that can control the

Iguanodon
large plant eater

Camptosaurus
plant eater

Diplodocus
the largest reptile

Ornitholestes
agile predator of
birds and mammals

Ankylosaurus
heavily armored
plant eater

Ctenacodon
first plant-eating
mammal with specialized
teeth for gnawing
like a rat

Early Eutherians
shrew-like ancestors of
placental mammals, which
scavenged and ate insects

Tyrannosaurus
giant flesh eater,
50 feet long,
20 feet high
and weighing
almost 8 tons

latter – like mammals and birds – also have to burn a lot of food when it's cold, not to *do* anything, just to maintain their temperature, what we call keeping warm. That needs a lot of oxygen. The reptiles, with their primitive lungs, just couldn't get enough.

And they were already on borrowed time. The winners of the future were living modestly among them, waiting for the right circumstances.

But it would be a long wait. The dinosaurs and the ferns and aquatic plants they fed upon were in a perfect, mutually supporting balance; only when the balance was severely disturbed did the newcomers find their chance.

Triceratops
horned plant-eating dinosaur

43

The mammals ... a community of staggering diversity

With the mammals a body plan with greater potential for life on land had evolved. Their supreme advantage lay in their adaptability to the widest range of climates, from the hottest to the coldest, from the equator to the pole.

This derived from their ability to control their body temperature. Mammals have a skin covered in hair and rich in oil glands for water repellence. Other glands supply sweat which evaporates to cool them. If they grow too cold, they can raise their fur to trap more air – it's as good as pulling on an extra sweater.

Ichthyornis
ancestor of modern birds

Notharctus
tree-living early primate, ancestor of lemur

Diatryma
giant "terror bird"

Bat
the only mammal to have mastered flight

Aegyptopithecus
tree-living primate earliest known ancestor of modern apes and humans

Sthenurus
ancestor of kangaroo

Eusmilus
saber-tooth tiger

Early Eutherians
shrew-like ancestors of placental mammals

Hyaenodon
carnivorous mammal

Plesiadapis
squirrel-like mammal, similar to ancestors of the primates

Glyptodon
ancestor of armadillo

44

The tree ferns had been supplanted by conifers and with the evolution of flowering plants had come a far greater diversity of vegetation. Forests and grassy plains, much as we know them today, provided the mammals with new opportunities for food and shelter. On the plains, herds of grazing animals led an uneasy existence with their predators. To survive, some evolved longer legs, tracing an evolutionary pattern like that of the modern horse. Others gained security with size. The forest canopy provided security and a wealth of leaves and fruit for the agile ancestors of the primates. Apart from the bat and the horse, all these forms are extinct.

Proper temperature control gave them a wonderful internal stability that led to the greatest development of all: a brain that was alert even in the coldest climates.

The offspring of such an animal requires constant warmth and could not therefore be left to develop inside an egg, where the temperature frequently varies and the waste products steadily accumulate until hatching. They now had to develop inside the mother, relying on her temperature-control and blood-purifying systems. Some of the sweat glands in the skin developed a new function – making milk to feed the newborn young.

As the mammals diversified on the land so the birds took every opportunity in the air. Their increasing command of the sky made them safe from predators on the ground and gave them access to the great variety of seeds, fruit and insects in the trees. They retained the reptilian egg but, being warm-blooded, were able to keep it warm.

Almost two billion years had passed since the creation of the first community of plant, animal and scavenger cells. In that time nature had created and acted on countless opportunities. The result . . . a community of staggering complexity.

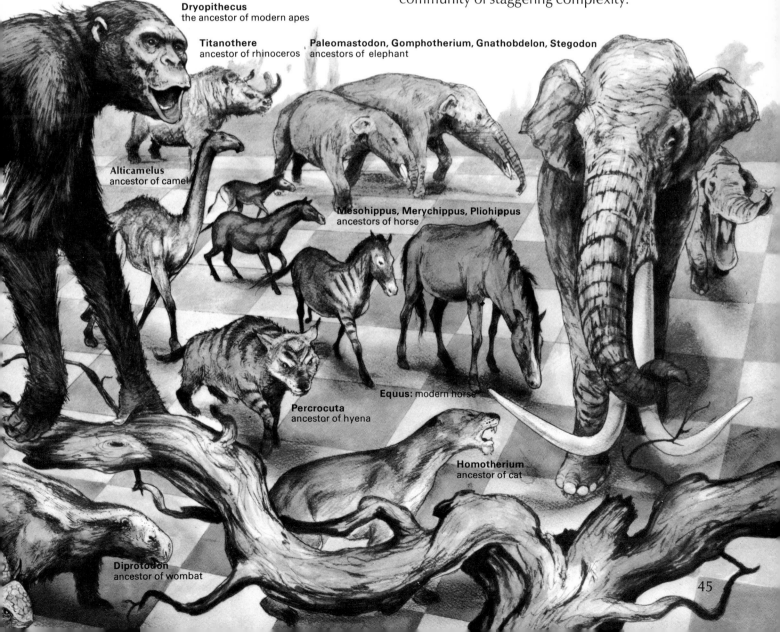

Dryopithecus
the ancestor of modern apes

Titanothere
ancestor of rhinoceros

Paleomastodon, Gomphotherium, Gnathobdelon, Stegodon
ancestors of elephant

Alticamelus
ancestor of camel

Mesohippus, Merychippus, Pliohippus
ancestors of horse

Equus: modern horse

Percrocuta
ancestor of hyena

Homotherium
ancestor of cat

Diprotodon
ancestor of wombat

Ramapithecus, ancestor of man
The earliest man-like ape lived near the edges of forests in Asia, Europe and Africa between 15 and 8 million years ago. His teeth and jawbone show that he ate small hard objects such as nuts and roots. He may have shuffled along in a squatting position with his hands free to pick up his food. To sleep and at times of danger he would have returned to the nearby trees. He was about the same size as a modern gibbon.

The life that led to man

As mammals diversified the different types evolved by increasing the efficiency with which they exploited their particular environments. Fangs for flesh eaters, strong running legs for grazers and so on. Some types were spectacularly successful, but as they became specialized so they became less adaptable to major changes in their environment. Only among primates, in the safety of the treetops, could more generalized improvements occur.

Up in the treetops you need keen sight, to spot food and enemies and to pick a fast escape route through a 3-D maze when danger looms. So eyes turned to the front of the head to better judge depth and distance. Color vision, lacking in most other mammals, was perfected. Primates whose DNA altered so as to make these changes were more successful. And bigger optical centers therefore became standard.

This improved efficiency of the optical center led to the further development of two other areas of the brain. One to process the input and one to control the output. Altogether: see, understand, act. Among primates there was a great increase in the pathways between the optical center and the centers for judgment and planning, and co-ordination of movement. It was no use seeing an escape route through a maze of branches if one of them was not going to support your weight!

Out of this increase in the brain's pathways came that special feature which distinguishes the primates from all other creatures – their intelligence. In fact the only difference between primates' brains and those of the rest of the mammals lies in the complexity of their pathways. For example, the human brain cell is not of itself smarter than, say, a pig brain cell; it just happens to be far more richly and densely interconnected with other brain cells. And that richness of interconnection provides the input that allows a human to think thoughts that never occur to a pig.

This increase in complexity led to enlargement of the frontal region of the brain – the "uncommitted" area that processes inputs from specialized areas such as the optical center, and that later, in man, would be concerned with such things as initiative, learning and above all concentration.

The steady shrinking of the strong bony ridges on the skull, which had given strength to the large jaws once necessary for defense, enabled the skull to change with the need for a larger brain. This produced the high forehead, which gets higher and higher the nearer the evolutionary path gets to man

Life in the treetops had another of those disadvantages that turn out to be advantages in the long run: it made the rearing of young difficult. Ground-based hunters, like lions or foxes, can afford to produce large litters of almost helpless young. When born they will be safe in their den and can learn about the world and each other while their parents stand guard.

But primate mothers who need mobility to range freely through the treetops can carry only one or two young inside at a time. What is more, the young primates must be born sufficiently mature and developed to hang on to their mothers and survive without the protection of a nest. To rear these few offspring successfully requires greater maternal care. Couple that care with the greater brain power of the primates and you can see the dawning of love and of the complex kind of communication that must have led up to the power of speech.

Treetop life had another bonus for some. To swing from branch to branch without falling calls for a good grip. And if your food includes grubs and fruit and nuts, you need pretty sophisticated finger-and-thumb action. If you drop a tasty morsel, it's a long way down to get it back. And for all of these things you need a marvelous coordination of hand and eye. All our basic skills as a toolmaker and tool user go back to the grip-and-dexterity days of our treetop ancestors.

There came a time about 10 million years ago when the climate became colder. The Ice Ages were approaching and the enormous forests that spread over most of Africa and well up into Europe began to retreat. Among the primates was Ramapithecus, the ancestor of man. He began to take advantage of the new opportunities down on the ground and open spaces. For him, and for us, it was the beginning of a great adventure.

Slow, weak, vulnerable . . . but thinking

The quarter-way humans who came down out of the trees when the approach of the Ice Ages began to threaten the forests couldn't afford to be picky about what they ate: grubs, roots, fruit, any small creature that came their way (and couldn't get out of it fast enough) . . . all of these were on the menu. In accepting such a wide diet they were competing with a large number of animals that had been living successfully on the ground for tens of millions of years. It was no easy start. Would you care to hunt rabbits in competition with packs of wild dogs? Or dig for roots against wild hogs with their long tusks and 400 pounds of muscle and bone? And remember – you can't run as fast as any other ground-living mammal, and to a cheetah or one of the other big cats or dogs you are just as succulent as any plump young buck.

It is interesting to see how other primates who have taken to the ground manage. Chimpanzees live for choice in scrub and brush and take to the trees when danger threatens. Gorillas live on the ground, but only in dense forest or thick mountain scrub. And baboons, who diverged from our evolutionary line about 30 million years ago, live in rigidly organized foraging packs with a very strict military-style discipline to govern their social relationships. None of these creatures went in for the aggressive hunting-pack style used so effectively by the dogs and some of the big cats.

None, that is, except the early humans – and even then it took them many millions of years to evolve a brain big enough to compensate for the lack of fangs, speed, and sheer brawn. The quarter-way humans of 10-to-5 million years ago certainly weren't up to it.

They lived a chimpanzee-like existence, never too far from trees or tall shrubs or escarpments where they could climb out of danger. Over that time span they began to evolve into two distinct kinds of creature whom we could call half-way humans. These are the two forms of Australopithecus.

One kind never made it more than half way; it became extinct about a million years ago and may have been killed off by the second kind. It was a sort of gorilla-man, with a gorilla-size brain. It could not walk perfectly upright and may have dropped back to all fours when moving any distance. To judge by its teeth it lived mainly on seeds and nuts and other small, hard food that needed grinding before it could be swallowed and digested. It was probably as hairy as any of the other apes.

The second kind of half-way human lies directly on our line of ancestry. It did not specialize in its diet, nor, to start with, did it go in for the spectacular increase in size that the first kind enjoyed. Nevertheless, over the same time span, 5-to-1 million years ago, it developed a brain that was at least half as large again as its gorilla-like cousins. (The fully human brain, by the way, is a bit more than twice as large again.)

These smaller, more chimp-sized half-way humans had many other features that bring them closer to the human line, even though they, too, could not walk perfectly upright as we do. For instance, although they began as scavengers and foodgrubbers, they soon took to more ambitious kinds of hunting and eventually could hunt up to quite long distances from their base areas.

To do that they could not rely on the sort of crude tools that chimps and gorillas fashion out of sticks and twigs and rocks at the moment of need – whatever happens to be lying around; they had to prepare tools in advance, perhaps a day or two in advance, and carry them out on their hunting forays. It takes a fairly sophisticated brain to achieve that.

Naturally such an amazing development does not happen alone; it goes hand in hand with many others. Language, for instance. Cooperative hunting by creatures that lacked the speed and power and teeth of dogs would have been difficult without the ability to communicate. Language was an enormous breakthrough. Nothing since has matched it for its power to deal with the outside world. "How shall we cross this river?" "Let's put stepping stones in it." "No, it's too deep. Let's walk upstream until we find a shallow place." "No, that'll delay us too much. Let's put that tree trunk over it." "We must test it first to see if it will bear the heaviest of us." And so on. The speakers of this dialogue take less than 15 seconds to perform four mental

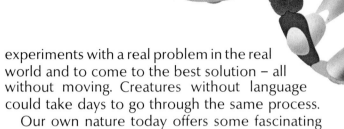

experiments with a real problem in the real world and to come to the best solution – all without moving. Creatures without language could take days to go through the same process.

Our own nature today offers some fascinating clues (and they are no more than clues) to the conflicts that may have stirred in those ancestors of ours as they first took to this perilous new path.

For instance, if we examine ourselves we can find two quite contradictory characteristics in the way we like to organize ourselves. On the one hand we seek after the tight military discipline that is so noticeable among some baboons, with their rigid male hierarchies.

On the other hand we also cherish the mother-father kind of family unit and the sort of even-handed "democracy" that is more characteristic of the hunting-dog pack. One possibility is that we began by moving toward the foraging way of life, out in the open, but were beaten to it by the baboons. Their DNA specialized for that way of life faster than ours; so they had the usual instant success that specialization brings. Our earliest ancestors then took a new direction, but not before a little militarism had been written into our nature.

At all events, it was during this time that we adopted the mother-father family unit as the basis of our way of life. The baboon type of organization, with females for a few dominant males only, did not offer enough motivation to bring *all* the males back from their long, arduous, and dangerous hunting forays; only the thought in each male's mind that *his* family was waiting back there and was depending on him could get him to do that.

Other human traits shown by these half-way folk included their habit of building crude lean-to shelters of twigs and branches; this may have been a night-time compensation for their loss of body hair – or rather, the shortening and thinning of hair that singles out humans from other apes. Also they dug holes for collecting water; and they collected salt instead of going out and foraging for it whenever they needed it, like other animals.

By about a million years ago this second type of half-way human made the transition to full human-ity. He stood upright, leaving his hands entirely free to fashion and hold tools, to carry things, and to manipulate them. Not surprisingly we call him Homo Erectus.

The sort of tools Homo Erectus made were far more potent than those of his ancestors. He made pointed wooden spears, which he may have tipped with poison as do today's Bushmen and Aborigines. He also made hand axes with axheads of stone and handles of wood. Most important of all, he discovered the art of making fire.

This last discovery led to two further break-throughs. Once he could cook his kill, he could seek much larger quarry. Primates cannot easily digest large muscle in the raw; cooking changed all that. Also, fire made it possible for him to survive in colder parts of the world and to withstand the colder seasons of the year more easily. Until this time his ancestors had been confined to the warm equatorial scrub and grasslands of eastern and north eastern Africa. But Erectus spread throughout Africa and then on to Europe and Asia.

In parallel with these developments came a massive increase in the size of the human brain. A million years ago the most intelligent of our ancestors had a brain a little more than half the size of ours. Almost all the extra capacity has gone into the front part of the brain, the seat of our intelligence.

In fact, the human brain was more than just the seat of intelligence, it had become the focus of evolution – the center from which all the major evolutionary advances of the future will spring.

In the continuing story of how the original matter of the universe has rearranged itself, our attention now turns away from DNA toward this new thing – the human mind, the place where that matter has at last become aware of itself.

Only you can ask why

While our DNA had been evolving toward increased finger-and-thumb dexterity, bigger brain size, and greater intelligence, the DNA in our nearest relations, the apes had also been changing.

The least like you, the gibbon, had specialized in moving fast through trees. The orangutan, much slower than the gibbon, had increased its size now that it was free from predators. On the ground a large group of gorillas had little to fear also, while the chimp had formed into large, noisy, gregarious family units, able to sound the alarm and make for the safety of the trees.

You are slightly closer to the chimp than to the other primates. And this similarity shows up in your DNA. If we take a single strand of human DNA and match it against a strand of chimpanzee DNA the difference is only 2.5 percent; and with the gorilla only a little more. And even in an area where you appear to have changed – walking upright – your DNA has not had the time to do more than a half job of it. We suffer constant trouble with our backbones, our sinuses and our hips, because their basic design still harks back far too strongly to the typical four-limbed walk of the apes.

In behavior too there are marked similarities between us and the apes. They have highly mobile faces, unlike the rigid masks of the other mammals. Tightly pressed lips, pouting, lip smacking, grinning, staring or averted eyes, and movement of the brow all express pleasure, puzzlement, fear, aggression or submission.

Adult gorillas, though very peace-loving, will drum their chests as a signal of challenge, and chimps love to produce plenty of noise by rhythmic hand clapping, stamping or beating a resonant tree in the jungle. And they all have distinct calls for warning or mutual contact. They are curious and playful; they love the young – those of others as well as their own – and frequently reassure each other by grooming or touching.

In all these respects and many others the difference between you and the apes is one of degree. What really marks you out from the apes began when humans developed language. The difference is really between two ways of understanding the world around us – two different kinds of intelligence. You use one kind as do the apes when you listen to a musical chord; that is, you don't hear single notes and consciously add them together, you actually hear the harmony as a whole. When you walk around a room, or construct a pattern, even if your eyes are focused on one element in it, your mind is conscious of the entire thing – again, as a whole.

Yet while you were reading that last paragraph you were using a very different sort of intelligence – the sort that works in a step-by-step sequence, the sort that constructs chains of logic and reason. So you have two kinds of intelligence: the kind that grasps things as a whole, and the kind that works step by step. We call the first kind holistic, the second kind sequential.

No other animal, not even our nearest cousins among the apes – the chimpanzees – has this dual type of intelligence so well developed. People whose speech centers, which depend on the sequential type of intelligence have been damaged are not able to construct sentences that are longer than ten words or so. Ten words, it seems is the most that they can grasp with their holistic intelligence; after that they lose the thread. It is fascinating to realize that although chimps have not developed the capacity for speech, they can be taught sign language, but cannot break the "ten-word" barrier!

It is this capacity for sequential thought that makes us the only animal capable of even asking the question "Where do I come from?"– let alone trying to answer it.

Gibbon
Lives in the tropical rain forests of southeast Asia. Swings from branch to branch and can walk with his hands in the air. Eats mostly fruit and leaves but also eggs and young birds. Lives in small groups with offspring dependent for 2 years. Brain is one-fourteenth the size of man's. Average lifespan: 10 years.

Man
Lives in all habitats. Stands upright leaving his hands totally free. Will eat vegetables and meat. Usually lives in small family units in permanent houses. Young are dependent for 15 years. Brain size is about three times that of the chimpanzee. Average lifespan: 77 years.

Orangutan
Only a very few survive in the tropical rain forests of Borneo and Sumatra. Swings slowly from branch to branch and walks on all fours. Eats mostly fruit. Lives a very solitary life. Lone males are common. Young are dependent for 6 years. Brain is one-third the size of man's. Average lifespan: 40 years.

[Gorilla] ...most of its life on the ground in lowland or mountainous forest of equatorial Africa. Swings in trees with support from legs, and uses all fours on the ground. Eats only bark, leaves, bamboo shoots, bananas and sugar-cane. Lives in groups of up to 40 with one dominant male. Sleeps on the ground and occasionally in trees. Young are dependent for 3 years. Brain is over one-third the size of man's. Average lifespan: 35 years.

Chimpanzee
Lives in tropical rain forests of Africa. Swings in trees, often using legs for support. All fours on the ground. Eats mostly fruit, leaves, seeds and bark. Lives in groups of two to twenty. Young are dependent for 2 years. The brain is about one-third the size of man's. Average life span: 40 years.

51

No ordinary predator

Between 400,000 and about 70,000 years ago Homo Erectus changed in so many ways that we have to consider him a new species: Homo Sapiens – the name we modestly call ourselves, the Wise Man.

The earliest member of this new human species – named Neanderthal after the German valley where his remains were first discovered – was short and stocky. Like the modern Eskimo he was adapted to live in the colder regions of a world in the grip of the ice ages.

He was probably the first man to wear clothing – to compensate for the lack of hair that Homo Erectus had bequeathed him. He made this clothing, and tents as well, from the skins of the animals he killed – everything from mammoths to small ponies.

He was also the first man to bury his dead with signs of reverence – that is, he was the first to show an awareness of a spirit world behind or beyond the material one that supplied his bodily needs. If you think that this spiritual aspect of our nature is what marks us off from the rest of the animal world, then Neanderthal is the first man we can be sure was truly human.

Though sheer brain volume is no hard-and-fast guide to intelligence, it is interesting to note that Neanderthal's brain was bigger than modern man's by an average ten percent. It used to be thought that he was wiped out by his more aggressive cousin (ourselves 40,000 years ago), but it seems just as likely that the two human strains interbred and merged around that time.

At all events, the successor to Neanderthal was Cro-Magnon man, well known for his habit of painting on the walls of caves. Actually, he lived mainly in small villages under tents of skin supported by mammoth bones – a way of life much like that of the American Indians.

He was taller than Neanderthal and much more recognizably like ourselves. He was much more like us, too, in his way of life. He probably wore crudely tailored skins and shod his feet with animal hide. He made highly sophisticated tools of bone and antler as well as of the traditional stone and wood; and they were far more specialized than those of Neanderthal – knives, scrapers, borers, fish-hooks, harpoons, and even tools for engraving.

With their help he fashioned ornaments and jewelry to high standards of craftsmanship. And the beauty and skill of his art, preserved miraculously for us in such caves as Lascaux and Altamira near the borders of what are now France and Spain, can still move us to wonder.

On the evolutionary line between the quarter-humans of 10 million years ago and ourselves, these artistic hunters are no more than a hairsbreadth away from us – if that. In physique and skill and intelligence all the evidence shows that they were identical to ourselves – all that truly separates us is 20 thousand years or so of cultural evolution: the long story of our growing numbers and the rising trade and civilization that supported the increase.

We who live amidst the luxurious amenities of the 20th century tend to think of the life of the hunter-foodgatherer as uncomfortable, half brutish, and very short. In fact, of all the ways in which humans have chosen to live, the life of the hunter-foodgatherer is probably the easiest of all. Even the Kalahari Bushmen, living in one of the least hospitable areas of the world, hunt, on average, only 2 hours a day, and never more than 32 hours a week. Yet they all eat as much protein as the average US citizen (and more than the Briton or the German) and in any Bushman community some 10 percent of the people are over 60 years of age. In short, they achieve a standard of living, of health, and of life expectancy comparable to that of ourselves in our industrial society; yet they do it without capital on a very short working week. It is little wonder that for 99 percent of our time on Earth we humans have lived the simple, rewarding, satisfying, and leisured life of the hunter and foodgatherer. The mystery is that we ever took to any other way of life.

Part of the explanation must lie in our rising numbers. When predators hunt their territory so much that their food supply begins to fail, there is a natural and inevitable reaction. Starvation and

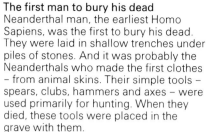

The first man to bury his dead
Neanderthal man, the earliest Homo Sapiens, was the first to bury his dead. They were laid in shallow trenches under piles of stones. And it was probably the Neanderthals who made the first clothes – from animal skins. Their simple tools – spears, clubs, hammers and axes – were used primarily for hunting. When they died, these tools were placed in the grave with them.

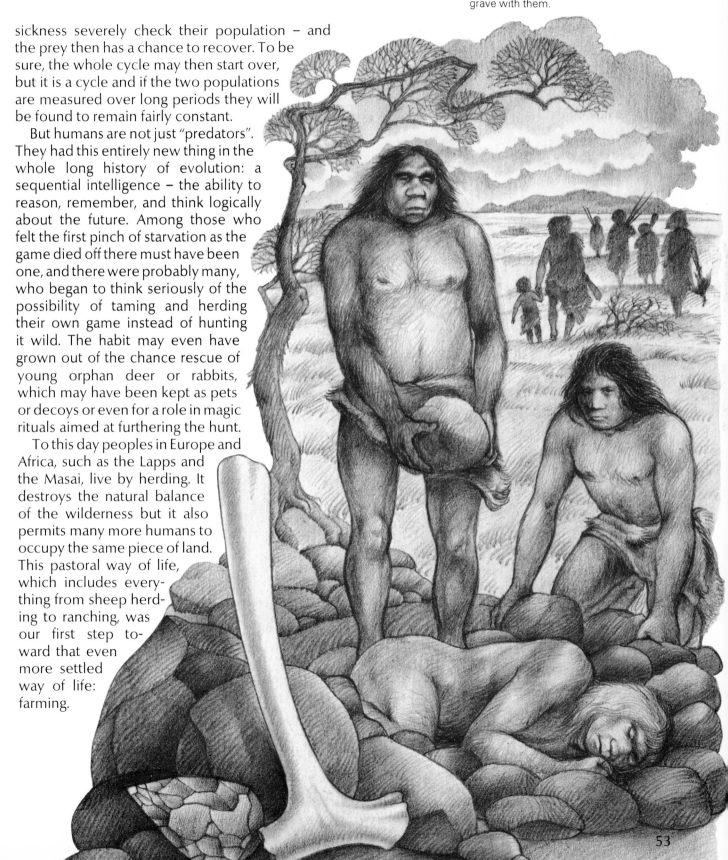

sickness severely check their population – and the prey then has a chance to recover. To be sure, the whole cycle may then start over, but it is a cycle and if the two populations are measured over long periods they will be found to remain fairly constant.

But humans are not just "predators". They had this entirely new thing in the whole long history of evolution: a sequential intelligence – the ability to reason, remember, and think logically about the future. Among those who felt the first pinch of starvation as the game died off there must have been one, and there were probably many, who began to think seriously of the possibility of taming and herding their own game instead of hunting it wild. The habit may even have grown out of the chance rescue of young orphan deer or rabbits, which may have been kept as pets or decoys or even for a role in magic rituals aimed at furthering the hunt.

To this day peoples in Europe and Africa, such as the Lapps and the Masai, live by herding. It destroys the natural balance of the wilderness but it also permits many more humans to occupy the same piece of land. This pastoral way of life, which includes every-thing from sheep herd-ing to ranching, was our first step to-ward that even more settled way of life: farming.

53

Adapting nature to his needs

It was probably our growing numbers that forced us around 10,000 years ago to adopt the settled life of the farmer. If it takes, say, 1000 acres to keep a hunter-foodgatherer, and 100 to satisfy a pastoralist, a farmer and his family can get by on less than 5 acres. Even more important, a farmer with wooden plows and oxen can till not 5 but 50 acres. He can produce a huge surplus to feed a big non-farming population. And all of them can amass goods and store grain – making them independent of the day-to-day vagaries of nature in a way the hunter-foodgatherer never can be.

Familiar? Isn't it exactly the sort of thing that happened when living cells first discovered the chlorophyll trick? Ultimately that revolution led to large, multicelled organisms. In a similar way this revolution led to large, multi-talented organizations – cities, states, nations . . . civilizations.

A more settled way of life
The hunter-foodgatherers eventually changed to a more settled lifestyle that could support a larger number of people. Cattle, pigs and goats were herded, using stockades to protect them from predators. The forest was cleared so that the ground could be tilled and the crops sown. Wild varieties of wheat, barley, millet, beans, lentils and peas were improved and made more productive by selection. Implements of stone, bone and wood helped in the harvesting and preparation of food crops. Decorated clay pots were used for storage and cooking.

55

Surpluses . . . specialists . . . civilization

What does a primitive farmer need in order to become more effective? A metal plow instead of a wooden one. Stout earthenware jars to keep grain dry and free of vermin. Someone to dig and operate ditches for irrigation or drainage. Someone to mill the grain. All of these are specialist services; and the specialists can exist only if the farmer can produce a surplus, enough food to feed them as well as himself.

Surpluses are attractive, especially to those who don't have them. Farmers were never long immune to either casual theft or the organized theft of war. The next necessity, then, was a police force and an army. By the time society reaches that state of organization it is getting too complex to manage on informal lines. In the early days you could say "Make me a good plow and I'll give you three sacks of grain at harvest"; but now there were getting to be too many people to operate that kind of simple barter system. They had to find a token that everyone could accept as being equal in value to so much grain or so many hours' work. And the token was money.

Money, being light and easily portable, soon promoted trade between areas where barter would have been impossible. With amazing speed (when you consider how slowly evolution had previously worked) a rich network of communications grew up, especially throughout Asia Minor and the Middle East – the cradle of most of these new developments.

There was intellectual evolution, too, to match these material changes. Greatest among them were the inventions of writing and of mathematics. Writing is the DNA of civilization – just as we might say that speech is its RNA. The spoken record is vulnerable. If someone forgets or changes a vital bit of a spoken record, the truth is forever lost – just as, right back at the beginning of life, when DNA had to do all the work of making protein and acting as the storehouse of inheritance, if it got damaged in use the record was lost forever. But a written record was safer and lasted longer and did not spontaneously erase itself or change – just like the safely zipped up coils of DNA in the cell nucleus.

There is no such counterpart to math, but it did give a new precision to our systems of knowledge. In money affairs it helped sort out the profitable ventures from the rest and so prevented valuable resources from being squandered. In time it was to help teach us a great deal about the stars, the universe, and the world much nearer home.

Each step along the path of knowledge opened up new possibilities of further advance. Certainly anything that promoted wealth made it possible for cities and towns to support ever greater numbers of specialists. Each new specialist, in turn, fed new knowledge and discovery back into the mainstream of civilization.

Like a complex living organism, the city became a container in which all the rich interplay of farming, trade, administration, law, banking, learning, entertainment . . . and a myriad other specialties generated ever greater powers and broader understanding. In a living organism enclosed in skin, what we call life is the bustle of chemical and physical interactions; in a city wrapped in bricks and mortar, it is the bustle of human interactions in all these different fields.

But, as we have seen, living organisms feed off one another. Cities and civilizations do the same. Thus, trade, which may have begun with the simple swapping of tools at a water hole, came to stretch, 600 years ago, from China to far-off Greenland via the Great Silk Road to the Mediterranean and then on by the old Viking routes.

And today there is no country in the world that does not trade some commodity, directly or indirectly, with every other country in the world. Along with the trade go new learning, new ideas, and new skills – an endless process of interchange and improvement.

The march of civilization has never been one smooth progress. Our own western civilization had an almost fatal jolt when Ancient Rome fell at the barbarian onslaught. For over a millennium we returned to earlier and much simpler modes of life: smaller cities, isolated kingdoms, fewer specialists, reduced food surpluses, and a greatly diminished volume of trade. Huge amounts of Greek and Roman learning were just forgotten.

Forgotten – but not lost. Like DNA in a dormant cell, that knowledge lay unused in libraries in the eastern half of the former Empire where it was later discovered and refined by Arab scholars. When Europe discovered that knowledge again, it led to a great resurgence of civilization that ultimately reached most parts of the globe – a resurgence, indeed, that is still going on.

A few centuries ago our civilization reached an exciting new stage – a set of mutations, if you like. It discovered a new basis to civilization: energy, instead of food surpluses – or rather, as well as food surpluses. Energy now became the chief basis for a new kind of civilization, industrial civilization.

Industrial civilization gave an enormous boost to the age-old processes at the heart of civilization. The sheer quantity of knowledge it generated led to a vast increase in the number of specialists who kept everything moving and working. This, in turn, led to a startling increase in the volume of communication. In our own time, both these processes are going forward at an ever-increasing rate, with no end in sight. In fact, we are at a point where we could say that the exchange of information is actually more important to the work of our civilization – even to its survival – than is the exchange of material things. Many have called this a second industrial revolution – an *information* revolution.

In devising this industrial way of life we behaved no differently from the very first cells that ever evolved in the soup of the primeval world. We took the easiest course. The earth had seemingly untold riches of fossil fuels and minerals, and we now had the technology to exploit them – just as the soup had seemingly untold riches of food for the first cells to live on.

Well, we know what happened to the cells. They ran out of riches and had to devise their own way of making them. And now our civiliz- ation is beginning to run up against the same sort of barrier.

The rich diversity of man

Long before we settled down as farmers we had spread to every part of the globe. Beginning about 500,000 years ago man had fanned out over Europe, Asia and Africa. Compared with other animals that is a truly fantastic rate of spread – especially when you remember that although we started as grassland hunters, we soon invaded forests, woodlands, and even the frozen lands of the Arctic north.

The small hunting groups and families that settled in the wake of these great tides of expansion did not move very far from their own particular locality. A person might live and die, never having moved outside a circle of 20 miles' radius. These circles in which people move also define the areas in which they can select their mates. In other words, although our species spread right around the world, its individual members quickly settled into a large number of more or less isolated breeding populations. What effect did that have on the human stock of DNA?

The DNA stock of any species inevitably gains variety through mutation. These mutations are molded by two opposing forces; in this respect we are no different from any other animal. One force is the natural selection of those mutations which are an advantage to a particular environment. Nothing can prevent this. If you keep two populations of a species apart for long enough, they will eventually evolve away from one another and turn into two subspecies and then into two separate species, no longer able to interbreed. The opposite force comes from cross breeding between two populations that are tending to go separate ways, mingling their DNA and preserving the ability to interbreed. During most of our time as a world species the first of these two forces was upper-most. Groups in various parts of the world became different from one another and developed separate stocks of DNA. But in the last millennium or two the tide has turned; interbreeding between the races is helping to preserve the rich diversity of our DNA stock for our species as a whole.

The differences between the races are mostly superficial – color, hair type, blood group, facial characteristics, stature, but probably they do all confer some advantage in particular environments. Take color, for instance. Early man was probably dark-skinned. As he spread out and settled in different parts of the world, his skin color gradually changed with the varying amounts of ultraviolet in the sunlight. A balanced quantity of ultraviolet is essential to all of us. It acts on the deeper layers of the skin, and produces vitamin D, which is absent from almost all foods except the livers of some fish. Too much vitamin D is as dangerous as too little. In tropical zones the ultraviolet radiation is very high; so a dark skin affords protection. In northern regions it is very low, because most of it has been filtered out during the sun's long journey through the atmosphere; so a light skin more easily absorbs the necessary quantity.

In this way the many shades of skin color around the world are suited to producing the right amount of vitamin D. There are some exceptions – the Eskimos, for example, are a dark-skinned northerly people, but they get all the vitamin D they need from their abundant supplies of fish. The Chinese, on the other hand, have lighter skin containing a special substance to reflect some of the sunlight while still absorbing enough for their Vitamin D.

These and other differences have led us to try to classify man into three main groups–the Mongoloids, the Negroids and the Caucasoids.

Negroid from Nigeria

Caucasoid from Europe

Negroid from Jamaica

Caucasoid from India

Mongoloid from China

59

You are related to everybody

You have two parents, four grandparents, eight greatgrandparents . . . and that's going back only three generations. Go back 30 generations or 750 years and you have amassed more than one billion direct-line ancestors. Impossible! Even the world population was not that large then. Of course, there must have been almost as much interbreeding among your ancestors as there was between them and everyone else's. Nevertheless, the calculation shows that we are all related to each other and so we share an enormous store of DNA.

The information which specifies your basic identity is encoded in your share of this DNA. The letters of the DNA alphabet do not concern us, but what is important is the information that these letters spell out in words, sentences, or even paragraphs; each describing some aspect of your body such as the color of your eyes and hair. These functional units of DNA we call genes.

Genes come in pairs; one half of each of your pairs of genes came from your father, the other half from your mother. Usually one gene in each pair shows itself more strongly than the other. This explains why you can look more like your mother than your father, or the other way about. In the same way you may look like your grandmother or grandfather or even more remote ancestors whose genes you carry.

Each new generation of individuals carries new combinations of old genes. It's as if each one of us is dealt a fresh hand of cards from an enormous pack that gets shuffled for each generation.

Of your thousands and thousands of genes 90 percent are virtually identical with those of all other humans (that is, the differences between them are so slight that the only person they worry is the transplant surgeon – they are the sort of difference that would make you reject anybody else's kidney or skin graft).

They are almost exactly the same for everyone because they are the genes that make us humans rather than any other animal or plant. Of the remaining 10 percent half will be identical in all other humans of your sex: they are the genes that make you either male or female. Only the last 5 percent will come in the many different varieties that make you yourself and no one else; they are the genes that specify your color, eyes, hair, features . . . and all the other characteristics that are exclusively and uniquely *you*.

If you were to look again at that "unique 5 per cent" and compare these genes with those of other members of your family, undoubtedly many would be exactly the same. Lest you should think this belittles your uniqueness, remember that there are many many thousands of genes within that 5 percent – so there's still plenty of scope for difference. Now if you were to compare your mother's and father's "unique 5 percents" you would see much more difference between them than there was between yours and those of your brother or sister. If your mother and father were born in different countries it is very unlikely that they are at all closely related and so their 5 percent will appear very different. If we take this to one extreme they may actually belong to different races, such as we have seen on the previous page. On the other hand, your mother and father might have been born in the same village, in which case it is possible that they are related and are therefore carrying many more of the same genes.

This would have been more true of the Middle Ages. Then most people only had the choice of a handful of potential partners in marriage – which meant that a great many genes were just recycling in one locality. But there has been such an increase in mobility since then, particularly in recent years, that most young people have a greatly increased choice of potential marriage partners. The result is an immense mingling of genetic material that was once kept quite separate.

Another result of such mingling, as any plant or animal breeder can tell you, is almost always to improve the vigor of the stock. There is even a name for it: hybrid vigor. You could also call it the Brotherhood of Man, for the mingling of our DNAs stops us from dividing into different species.

The differences that help to make you

In one way human beings have always been more vulnerable than any other animal; we produce children that take 15 years or more to become mature enough to fend for themselves. All that time they need the devoted care of both parents, who therefore have to stay together and not seek new and different experiences with other partners. Yet we have always been creatures that love novelty and experiment, full of curiosity, continually seeking new experiences. How were these two features reconciled?

The answer was to make the difference between the parents – that is, their sexuality – exciting and rewarding in itself, quite apart from its role in producing the next generation. Humans enjoy sex more often and in more different ways than any other animal. And the difference, even between us and our closest relatives among the primates, is not just one of slight degree; it is vast.

Only something so basic could bond together two such intelligent and self-aware creatures as the human female and the human male.

Man and woman . . .
different needs . . . different demands

The differences between men and women are quite practical and down-to-earth in their origins. To understand that we have to think back to the days on the African plain when those quarter-way humans were first beginning to separate out from the rest of the apes.

In those days there was much less difference between the sexes; both probably foraged for food, and the young were materially dependent for perhaps only a year or two. But as this creature took to hunting and gained in intelligence, the gap between male and female gradually began to widen.

Bigger intelligence, bigger brain. That was a problem for the female; for the bigger the brain, the tighter the fit of the baby's head between the bones of the pelvic girdle at birth. This was partly resolved by having the baby born at an earlier stage than was usual among primates; and it was further eased by increasing the size of the female hip girdle (and even so, the fit is still tighter than in other primates).

To avoid hitting her hip when swinging an arm, the woman's elbow had to be further offset than a man's. This made her less adept at throwing; and her wider hips made her less capable as a sprinter or distance runner. So she would be a less efficient hunter than the male. Also, her baby – born premature by former standards – now needed much longer nurturing.

With the adoption of hunting came a distinct division of labor. Different roles were almost forced upon the two sexes – the man becoming the hunter, the woman the home-based food-gatherer and baby rearer.

At the same time permanent bonds between males and females developed. These helped the female during childbirth when she was at her most dependent and ensured that her children were protected and supplied with food. Such pairing also promoted trust among the males. They no longer had to compete for the attentions of the females in a promiscuous band, and felt secure enough to team up for long hunting expeditions.

The male and female were now apart more than before, so the sexual differences began to play an important role in reinforcing the bond and bringing the male back home, whatever excitement the wider world might offer. Unlike any other mammal the human female has developed the ability to enjoy sex at any time, even when she is pregnant. In fact those changes that occur in other primates, which excite the male only at that time when the female is able to conceive (for example, smell and coloration) have almost completely disappeared in human females.

Walking on their hind legs also changed the sexual preferences of humans. Other primates usually couple in the same way as dogs, where the male mounts the female from behind. Humans, with their upright gait, find face-to-face contact easier. Although the female chimpanzee and gorilla sometimes lie on their backs with the male squatting between their legs, the males never lie on the female's body as humans do. Face-to-face sex probably resulted from the natural resting positions of humans and it must have made the relationship even closer.

Along with this change to frontal sex, it is possible that the female's breasts swelled to resemble the two buttocks that other primate females present to the males before copulation. And their faces became more delicate, their lips more rounded. In contrast, the male beard acquired a distinct pattern. As both sexes lost body hair, skin-to-skin contact became more exciting than fur-to-fur. And the woman's clitoris (something like a tiny concealed penis not far from the vagina) became extremely sensitive and played a greater role in her enjoyment of sex. Gentle friction on both the penis and the clitoris can produce waves of high blood pressure resulting in the most intense sensation of physical pleasure – the orgasm.

Such, then, were the ways in which nature cemented the bond between parents so as to furnish the young with the secure and all-providing family it needed for so much longer than the young of other species.

Any human who tended toward the older ape patterns of behavior and body plan was less attractive to his or her partner. And the female had more at stake. If she failed to lure her partner back from the long and arduous hunting trip, she and her youngsters were likely in trouble. In short, such tendencies to revert, or not to change with the rest of the species, were soon bred out.

However, despite their common responsibility for their children, the two sexes had slightly different needs of each other – and the survival of the species as a whole placed different demands on each. The difference sprang both from their separate biological functions, and from their newly divergent roles.

The women were more important to the survival of the species than the men. A lot of men could die before the fertility rate even began to drop; not so the women. If somebody had to do the risky, foolhardy, or dangerous thing to help the group out of some difficulty it had better be the young men. Much better for the women to be the more sensible, cautious, thinking-ahead sort of people who would spot snags and pitfalls well in advance.

Because the young men were more exposed to the possibility of death, those groups in which they mated early with girls of their own age were vulnerable, and were less successful than groups in which young girls mated with older men. This second kind of group had two further advantages. The older men tended to be the survivors of past dangers, both of hunting and of tribal politics; theirs were the

sort of characteristics that confer success on their offspring. And the females had more fertile years ahead of them and could enjoy them in greater security.

Naturally, such girls were less attracted by their menfolk's physical charms than by their status; while for men the attraction was youth and the sort of physical beauty that goes with robust health. Groups in which such preferences operated were more successful than other groups and so their standards became the human norm.

Many of the other common differences between men and women were established during those 600,000 years of hunting and foodgathering; our mere 10,000 years of farming and city life have barely been enough to change such deep-rooted characteristics. For instance, as roaming hunters, the menfolk would be superior at making and using tools – especially those for hunting – and at mental mapmaking. They were taller, speedier and physically stronger. Their life was divided between bouts of extreme exertion at hunting, and long lazy days of relaxing, storytelling, dancing or just sleeping.

The woman's life as a foodgatherer was more regular. While in most hunting tribes the men hunt in small bands or alone, the women go foodgathering in large, chattering groups. The men must be ready for the game whenever it moves; but plants don't dictate the play like that, so the women have a more ordered and fixed routine.

As the hunter, a man matured physically more quickly, while as the child-rearer a woman matured earlier in her intelligence and emotions. She was more verbal, logical and sociable than the average man. Women also needed more stamina than men, for the demands of child care are potentially daylong and nightlong.

It may have been that the males were particularly dominant among our very earliest ancestors, but, as mankind evolved, the female came to play an increasingly strong role in the direction of affairs.

Not unnaturally many of the attributes that evolved to strengthen and maintain that life-long bond between parents in the hunting group, remain just as valuable in today's circumstances.

Love is learned early in life

All living things pass on a kind of survival kit to the next generation; usually, as with a bird's ability to build a nest, it is contained in the top-security package of their DNA. Some creatures, especially those with a rudimentary intelligence, pass on a few useful extras by example – chimps show their young how to poke twigs into termite heaps to extract the succulent insects inside; but more important, a baby chimp will learn from its mother how to communicate and love.

With humans learning is even more vital. Our DNA supplies us with a body, a mind, and a few basic programs; how we develop them and apply them depends entirely on what is passed on to us from the learning of earlier generations – what we call cultural inheritance – and on whether we are introduced to that learning in the right order, at the right time, and in the right way.

Cats bring their kittens out into the sunlight at a specific moment after birth. If this moment is missed, they will be blind for the rest of their lives. Human babies have set moments of learning, too.

As a baby you must be lifted, cuddled, talked to, smiled at, teased and played with. Later you must be read to, rewarded, corrected, reasoned with – often with endless patience. Among your fellows you must learn to play roles you may later take up in earnest: cops and robbers, doctors and nurses, and mothers and fathers. Later still you must loosen the close ties with your parents before you can build new relationships. You may need to rebel and fight, forgive and make up, many times, before you finally leave to face the adult world with an open, receptive mind, trying many novel things before you make any final choices.

A model person who came through all these phases without a hitch, might be idealistic, generous, compassionate and selfless. A person who missed out somewhere along the line might show the negative side of those traits and seem self-centered, dogmatic, introspective and antisocial. Most people, however, are a strange mixture of positive and negative traits. The model person and the absolutely loveless one are both as rare as June snowflakes.

The laws we have made about love

We all have dragons to kill. There's a great deal in our inheritance that we have to suppress or reinforce so as to be able to live more harmoniously with each other. Our DNA evolved so as to prepare us for living in small groups beneath crude shelters in a subtropical grassland. But as our numbers grew, we had to impose different codes of behavior to ensure survival. For a group to remain strong and vigorous, group loyalties and the bond between parents had to be reinforced.

Among the earliest codes must have been those designed to prevent in-breeding. Almost all societies, for example, forbid brother to mate with sister, father with daughter, or mother with son. To a lesser extent cousins may not be allowed to marry cousins, nor uncles and aunts their nephews and nieces. Such mating greatly increases the chance of inherited abnormalities and premature death.

Such rules also helped to create a harmonious society, because they promoted marriages – and therefore friendly cooperative relationships – among larger groups.

Later, as we began to live in even larger groups – towns and cities – small group loyalties were less vital to survival. But in that wider society, with its new diversions and opportunities, the bond between parents was at greater risk. Yet it was now even more important for the protection and upbringing of children. So new codes of behavior were introduced, designed to lessen the conflict between our sexuality and our need to live ordered lives within the community. For example, in some societies the taboo on physical contact with strangers results in elaborate apologies for even the most innocent of accidental brushes. And even the less inhibited behavior permitted between friends and relatives is governed by complex rules –handshakes, mouth to cheek kisses, and so on.

Many of the traditional laws, taboos, myths and legends are keyed to the deep conflicts that come with adolescence and young adulthood. Adolescence begins when DNA triggers off major changes in our physical and mental makeup. Those changes generate feelings that will never be experienced with such intensity again – idealism, ambition, romance, adventure and the urge to experiment.

The young male with his hunting, roving nature is less likely than the female to take seriously the responsibility of producing offspring. Many societies have devised complicated rituals and initiation ceremonies that must be performed before the young can take their places with the adults. To prepare for this transition, children are told stories and legends early in life, later to be reinforced by religious and community law. They tell of people who must undertake impossible missions, face death in a hundred forms, suffer untold hardships and privations, all for a remote but glittering prize.

There are many legends the world over that tell of a beautiful maiden imprisoned by a dragon. The heroic young man who rescues her must prove that he is fit to court her by undergoing near-impossible ordeals. Finally, against overwhelming odds, he slays the dragon and carries the maiden off to "live happily ever after." The love they then feel, after such long postponement, was considered nobler, purer and higher than it would have been if they had sought quicker and easier satisfaction.

Sex as an act of love

In the animal world the act of sex appears to be mainly functional; it precedes the generation of new offspring, usually occuring only when the female is fertile. But human evolution has turned this largely instinctive act into one of the most important and intense sources of pleasure in our lives. And because its evolutionary purpose was to strengthen the bond between parents and keep them together for the rearing of a family, it can be most rewarding between long-term partners.

In fact, it can be so much more rewarding that the pleasure reaches far beyond the immediate physical sensation to a region that borders on the magical. Nothing else allows us so direct a way to communicate with the one we love. For this essentially simple act can develop subtleties and powers that are awe-inspiring; not a sexual act, but truly an act of love.

Sex makes you unique

The wonder with which we have surrounded sex does not in any way obscure or frustrate its basic function, which is to mingle the DNA from two members of the same species and thus to try out different combinations of genes. Each creature is a living test bed for a particular combination of genes. Any gene that has mutated and happens to convey an advantage will promote the success of the individual that possesses it.

Success might be measured in terms of the number of descendants that an individual leaves. If the gene's advantage is maintained over several generations it will become part of the common heritage of that population and eventually the species – such is the mechanism of evolution.

Here is how the system works. If all the DNA from just one of your cells was pulled out into one long strand it would measure almost two yards. In that length you would find the multitude of genes that specify every detail of your body. To fit that enormous length into the nucleus of a cell calls for some very fine packaging. The DNA is coiled several times, as the picture shows, to get it small enough. In fact the length is now reduced to about the thickness of this letter I. This tiny length is then cut into 46 even smaller lengths called chromosomes, each one containing thousands of genes.

The chromosomes appear in pairs. Each pair has its characteristic shape and size, but the two members of each pair look very alike and carry identical or very similar genes. An exception is the pair of chromosomes that determine sex. Men have one very short Y chromosome paired up with a normal-sized X chromosome. Women have a pair of identical-looking X chromosomes. So you have 23 pairs of chromosomes, one member of each pair from your mother and the other from your father. For every gene on one chromosome (except the X, Y pair)

there is an equivalent one on the other chromosome of the pair. This means you have *two* copies of each of the many thousands of genes. Together the two genes of a pair control a single process in the cell, such as that which makes eye color.

The cells that become sex cells–the egg of the female and the sperm of the male–are quite different since each contains only 23 chromosomes, one of each of the different pairs. The set of 23 is produced from the set of 46 by a special process. In effect, one member of each of the 23 pairs is selected at random from the normal set. Your father had 23 chromosomes from his father (your grandfather) and a similar set from his mother (your grandmother). He passed 23 onto you, but it was a matter of chance from which grandparent each chromosome came. A further complication is that when sex cells are produced the chromosomes often exchange parts so that you probably have chromosomes that are partly from one grandparent and partly from the other.

The X and Y chromosomes are a little different. Half the sperm cells get a Y chromosome and the rest get an X, but all female egg cells will get an X chromosome. When a sperm and egg join together at fertilization the two sets of 23 make up the full complement of 46 chromosomes. If the sperm was carrying the Y chromosome the baby will be a boy; if it carried an X, a girl.

That's quite straightforward, but why are two brothers or two sisters different instead of looking identical as some twins do? This is because although they get half the genes from their father and half from their mother, each child gets quite different, random, proportions from the four different grandparents.

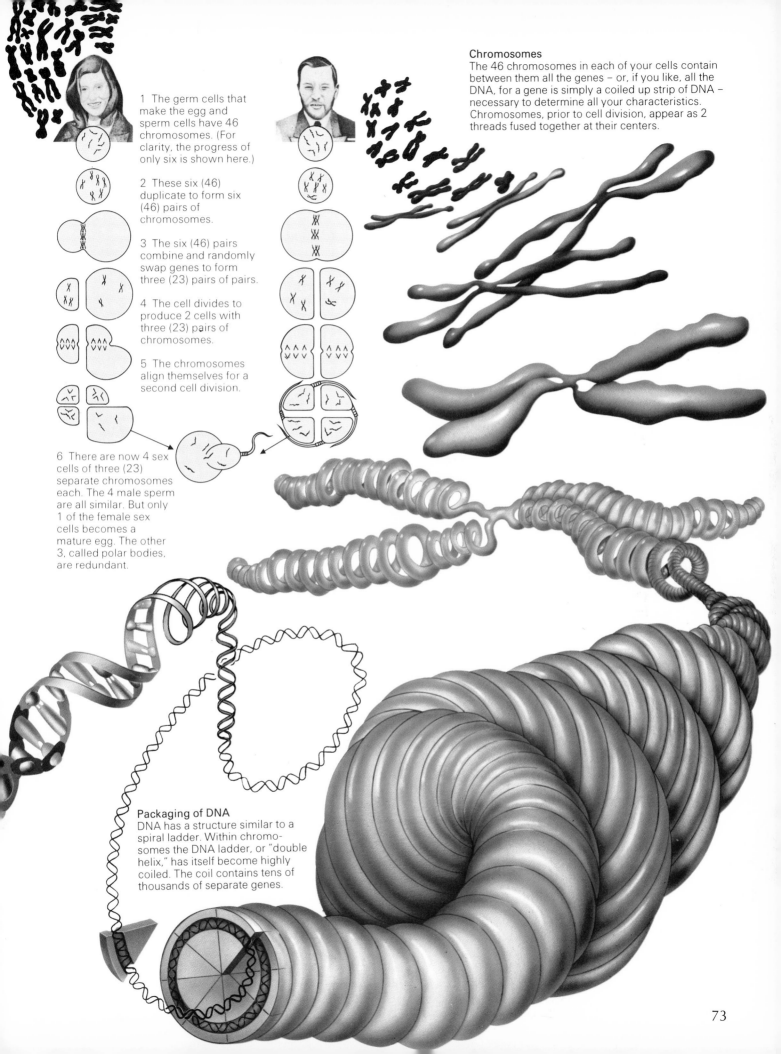

1 The germ cells that make the egg and sperm cells have 46 chromosomes. (For clarity, the progress of only six is shown here.)

2 These six (46) duplicate to form six (46) pairs of chromosomes.

3 The six (46) pairs combine and randomly swap genes to form three (23) pairs of pairs.

4 The cell divides to produce 2 cells with three (23) pairs of chromosomes.

5 The chromosomes align themselves for a second cell division.

6 There are now 4 sex cells of three (23) separate chromosomes each. The 4 male sperm are all similar. But only 1 of the female sex cells becomes a mature egg. The other 3, called polar bodies, are redundant.

Chromosomes

The 46 chromosomes in each of your cells contain between them all the genes – or, if you like, all the DNA, for a gene is simply a coiled up strip of DNA – necessary to determine all your characteristics. Chromosomes, prior to cell division, appear as 2 threads fused together at their centers.

Packaging of DNA

DNA has a structure similar to a spiral ladder. Within chromosomes the DNA ladder, or "double helix," has itself become highly coiled. The coil contains tens of thousands of separate genes.

One and one make one

There are about 50 trillion cells in your body; they all grew from one cell. They perform such an immense variety of tasks that even to list them would take over a dozen closely written books as thick as this. Yet all the information necessary to build them and get them in the right places and in sufficient numbers – all that was contained in two millionths of a millionth of an ounce of DNA, half from your mother, half from your father. Somehow,

too that same tiny package contained the information that determines how you walk, how quick you think, whether you're good at math or music or mechanics . . . even whether you are cheerful or dour by nature. People spend a lifetime studying these things and still they retain a sense of wonder at these marvels.

The adventure begins when the mother-to-be sheds one egg, occasionally more, from one of her

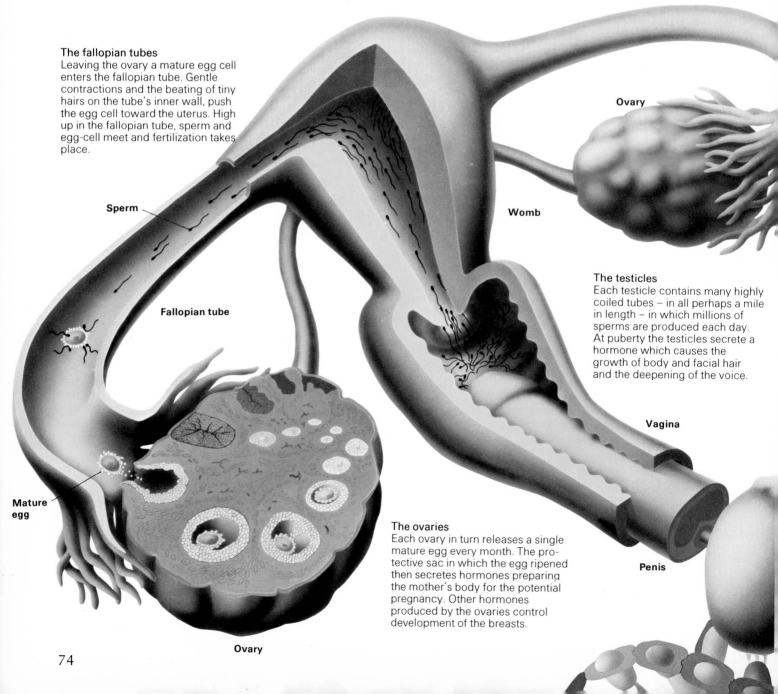

The fallopian tubes
Leaving the ovary a mature egg cell enters the fallopian tube. Gentle contractions and the beating of tiny hairs on the tube's inner wall, push the egg cell toward the uterus. High up in the fallopian tube, sperm and egg-cell meet and fertilization takes place.

Sperm

Fallopian tube

Mature egg

Ovary

Ovary

Womb

The testicles
Each testicle contains many highly coiled tubes – in all perhaps a mile in length – in which millions of sperms are produced each day. At puberty the testicles secrete a hormone which causes the growth of body and facial hair and the deepening of the voice.

Vagina

Penis

The ovaries
Each ovary in turn releases a single mature egg every month. The protective sac in which the egg ripened then secretes hormones preparing the mother's body for the potential pregnancy. Other hormones produced by the ovaries control development of the breasts.

two ovaries. They are shed alternately from each ovary, at about 28-day intervals. If the egg is not fertilized by a sperm, it passes down a long tube to the womb and then on out through the vagina. The lining of the womb, which thickens and fills up with a rich supply of blood vessels ready to accept the fertilized eggs, then breaks down, producing the monthly loss of blood known as menstruation.

To be fertilized the egg must meet the sperm

The seminal vesicles
The seminal vesicles produce a fluid, which joins with the fluid from the prostate, envelops the sperm and transports it out of the penis. It acts as the sperms' energy source on their journey toward the egg.

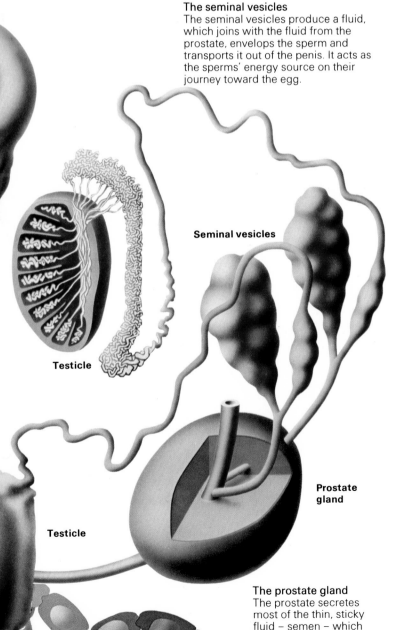

Seminal vesicles

Testicle

Testicle

Prostate gland

The prostate gland
The prostate secretes most of the thin, sticky fluid – semen – which surrounds and maintains the sperm.

in the tube between the ovary and the womb. The sperms start their journey in the vagina, when the man has an orgasm and ejaculates about a thimbleful of semen there. This semen consists of about 350 million individual sperms, all floating about in a sticky translucent fluid that is rich in sugars (for energy).

The sperms come from the testes; and the fluid comes from the other glands on the way to the outside world. The testes work on the safety-in-numbers principle. Theoretically only one sperm is needed to fertilize an egg; so the testes produce about 350 million for each ejaculation! Naturally quality suffers. About a quarter of the sperms never even start to swim. And of those that do, about one-seventh have some abnormality – two heads or short tails or some defect of that sort. But never mind, there are still about 250 million viable sperms ready to start the long journey toward the egg.

The sperms are so small that the eight inches from the vagina to the waiting egg cell are like four long miles to a man. Although they thrash their tails vigorously they are slow, inefficient swimmers and are very likely to set off in the wrong direction. Also the vagina is slightly acidic which does not suit the sperms half so well as the slightly alkaline film that covers the wall of the womb and fallopian tubes. Sperms obviously need some assistance if they are going to reach their goal. Semen contains substances which stimulate the muscular wall of the womb to ripple with movement. These waves of contraction will carry at least a few thousand sperms to the openings of the two egg tubes, but only about half will find themselves in the same tube as the waiting egg cell. It is only now that their active swimming movement helps them to tunnel away at the protective coat of the egg cell. Fertilization is achieved as soon as one has penetrated the membrane which suddenly becomes hardened against all the rest. Then the 23 chromosomes from the sperm match up with the 23 in the egg and the DNA in them is ready to go to work, specifying every physical detail of the new baby as it grows.

It divides, and divides and divides . . .

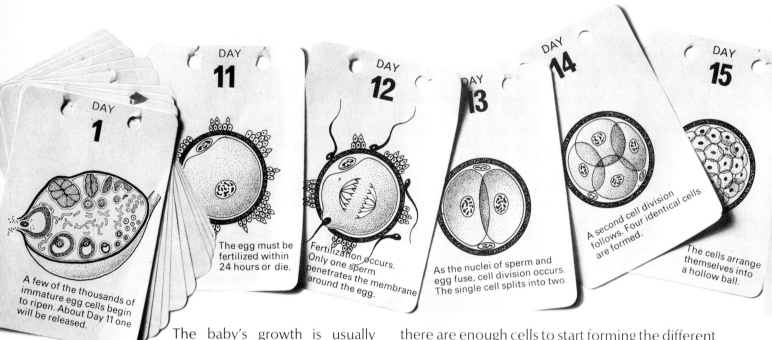

DAY 1
A few of the thousands of immature egg cells begin to ripen. About Day 11 one will be released.

DAY 11
The egg must be fertilized within 24 hours or die.

DAY 12
Fertilization occurs. Only one sperm penetrates the membrane around the egg.

DAY 13
As the nuclei of sperm and egg fuse, cell division occurs. The single cell splits into two.

DAY 14
A second cell division follows. Four identical cells are formed.

DAY 15
The cells arrange themselves into a hollow ball.

The baby's growth is usually dated from the moment the egg starts to ripen in the mother's ovary; that is also the time when her previous menstrual period ended, so it's an easy date for her to calculate. The ripened egg can be fertilized at any time between the 12th and the 20th day; here we assume the 12th.

When the two sets of DNA have come together in the egg – or embryo as it must soon be called – the egg splits into two cells. Occasionally these come completely apart. Then each one may grow into a full-term baby; and because they have identical DNA, they will be identical twins. (Non-identical twins occur when the mother produces two eggs simultaneously and both are fertilized by different sperm.)

For three days the fertilized egg drifts down the tube toward the womb, all the time dividing so that a little cluster of cells, like a microscopic mulberry, forms. This reaches the womb, whose lining has once again thickened and become enriched with blood vessels ready to support an embryo. After a few more cell divisions there are enough cells to start forming the different elements of the embryo baby. Most of them migrate outward to form the outer wall of a hollow sphere; the rest assemble in a mass at one end of the sphere, which after a few days becomes imbedded in the lining of the womb.

The outside of the sphere grows rapidly, digesting the lining of the womb to feed the mass of cells inside the sphere which will grow into the actual embryo. The invasion of the feeding cells into the lining of the womb continues but will stabilize and form the placenta – a spongy plate of flesh densely networked with blood vessels.

The developing embryo is connected to the placenta by the umbilical cord. This becomes the sole attachment and life-line, from the embryo to its mother. Through the umbilical cord, via the placenta, all the food and oxygen vital to the growing embryo are absorbed from the mother's blood, while waste matter travels in the other direction. By now, the amniotic sac–a large, fluid-filled bag–has formed a protective membrane around the baby.

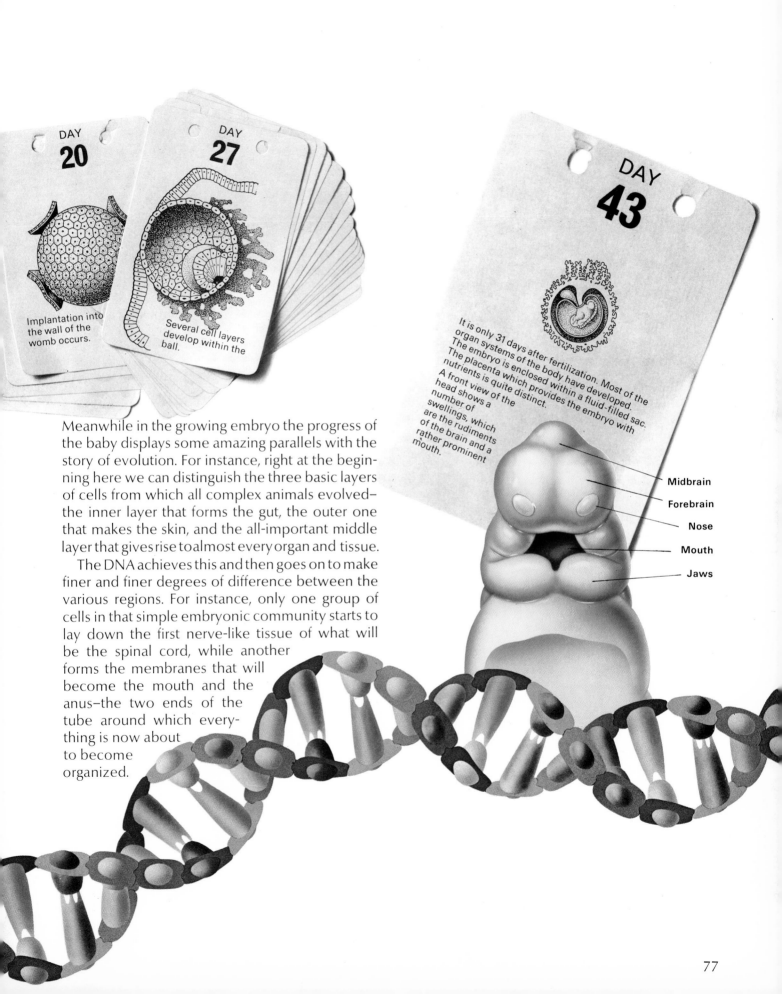

DAY 20

Implantation into the wall of the womb occurs.

DAY 27

Several cell layers develop within the ball.

DAY 43

It is only 31 days after fertilization. Most of the organ systems of the body have developed. The embryo is enclosed within a fluid-filled sac. The placenta which provides the embryo with nutrients is quite distinct. A front view of the head shows a number of swellings, which are the rudiments of the brain and a rather prominent mouth.

Midbrain

Forebrain

Nose

Mouth

Jaws

Meanwhile in the growing embryo the progress of the baby displays some amazing parallels with the story of evolution. For instance, right at the beginning here we can distinguish the three basic layers of cells from which all complex animals evolved—the inner layer that forms the gut, the outer one that makes the skin, and the all-important middle layer that gives rise to almost every organ and tissue.

The DNA achieves this and then goes on to make finer and finer degrees of difference between the various regions. For instance, only one group of cells in that simple embryonic community starts to lay down the first nerve-like tissue of what will be the spinal cord, while another forms the membranes that will become the mouth and the anus—the two ends of the tube around which everything is now about to become organized.

The heart of a fish . . .
the grip of a monkey

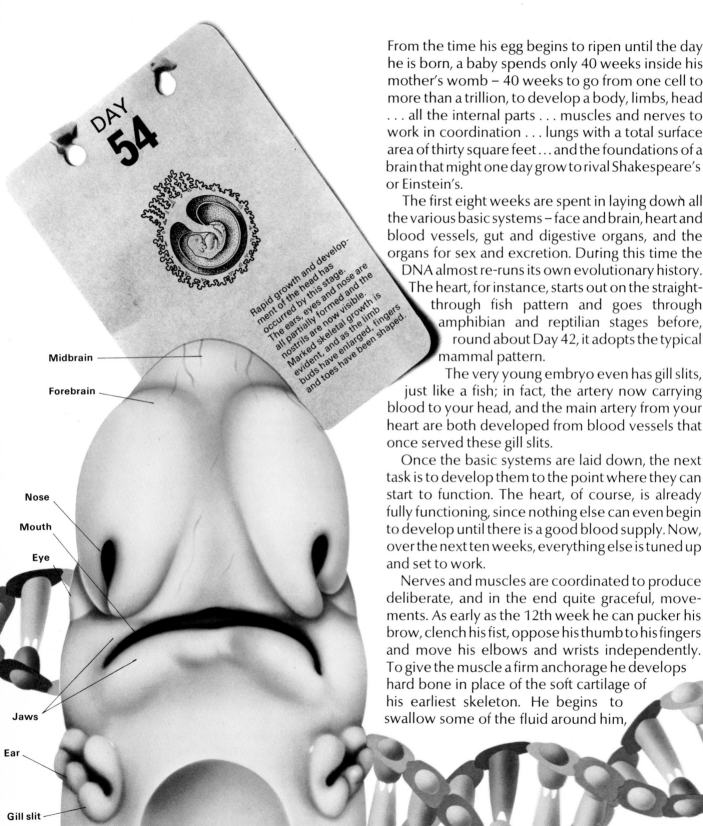

DAY 54

Rapid growth and development of the head has occurred by this stage. The ears, eyes and nose are all partially formed and the nostrils are now visible. Marked skeletal growth is evident, and as the limb buds have enlarged, fingers and toes have been shaped.

Midbrain

Forebrain

Nose

Mouth

Eye

Jaws

Ear

Gill slit

From the time his egg begins to ripen until the day he is born, a baby spends only 40 weeks inside his mother's womb – 40 weeks to go from one cell to more than a trillion, to develop a body, limbs, head . . . all the internal parts . . . muscles and nerves to work in coordination . . . lungs with a total surface area of thirty square feet . . . and the foundations of a brain that might one day grow to rival Shakespeare's or Einstein's.

The first eight weeks are spent in laying down all the various basic systems – face and brain, heart and blood vessels, gut and digestive organs, and the organs for sex and excretion. During this time the DNA almost re-runs its own evolutionary history. The heart, for instance, starts out on the straight-through fish pattern and goes through amphibian and reptilian stages before, round about Day 42, it adopts the typical mammal pattern.

The very young embryo even has gill slits, just like a fish; in fact, the artery now carrying blood to your head, and the main artery from your heart are both developed from blood vessels that once served these gill slits.

Once the basic systems are laid down, the next task is to develop them to the point where they can start to function. The heart, of course, is already fully functioning, since nothing else can even begin to develop until there is a good blood supply. Now, over the next ten weeks, everything else is tuned up and set to work.

Nerves and muscles are coordinated to produce deliberate, and in the end quite graceful, movements. As early as the 12th week he can pucker his brow, clench his fist, oppose his thumb to his fingers and move his elbows and wrists independently. To give the muscle a firm anchorage he develops hard bone in place of the soft cartilage of his earliest skeleton. He begins to swallow some of the fluid around him,

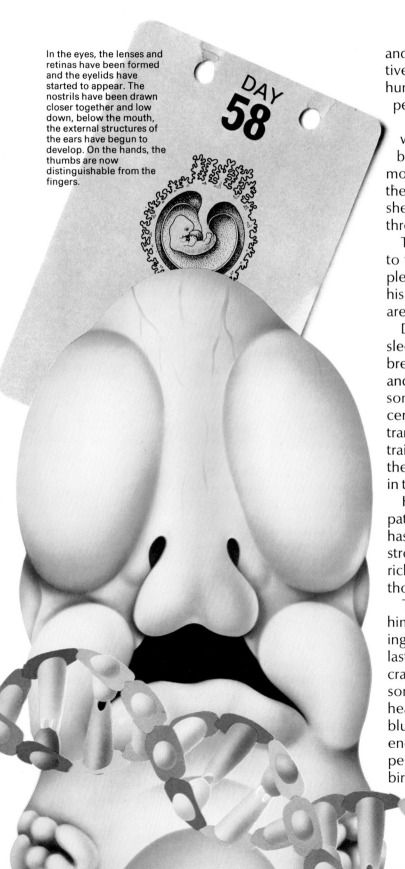

In the eyes, the lenses and retinas have been formed and the eyelids have started to appear. The nostrils have been drawn closer together and low down, below the mouth, the external structures of the ears have begun to develop. On the hands, the thumbs are now distinguishable from the fingers.

DAY
58

and its passage through his gut helps the digestive organs develop. By this time his face is not just human, it is recognizably that of an individual person; he may even show a family likeness.

Near the end of the fourth month he reaches a weight of 4 ounces and a length of 7 inches – too big to fit inside the protective girdle of his mother's hip bones. Her stomach begins to show the first swelling as he rises out of it. By the time she begins to feel his movements he is half way through his fetal life.

The second half of his time inside her is devoted to the finishing touches that will fit him for complete bodily independence – especially increasing his size and weight. And the final sophistications are added to all his functioning systems.

During the fifth and sixth months he begins to sleep and waken just like a newborn child. He breathes the fluid around him, which helps exercise and develop his growing lungs. He gets hiccups, sometimes for half an hour– and his mother can certainly feel it! He responds to noise and vibration transmitted through her stomach, such as car or train noises or a tap filling the bathtub while she is in the water. He swims a lot, often turning somersaults in the fluid.

He still has a short stretch of the evolutionary path to tread, too. For instance, at seven months he has the powerful grip of a baby monkey – far stronger than he will have at birth. He also grows a rich, downy fur, which may still be there at birth, though it falls out soon after.

Toward the end he adds a lot of fat to insulate himself against the cold he will encounter on leaving the all-enveloping warmth of the womb. In the last few weeks he literally begins to outgrow his cramped quarters. He can no longer squirm and somersault the way he used to, but now settles head down. That is the best position, too; his head is blunt and round, and it is the same circumference as his shoulders and buttocks, so it is perfectly fitted to blaze the trail down the birth canal.

It's hard to leave one world for another

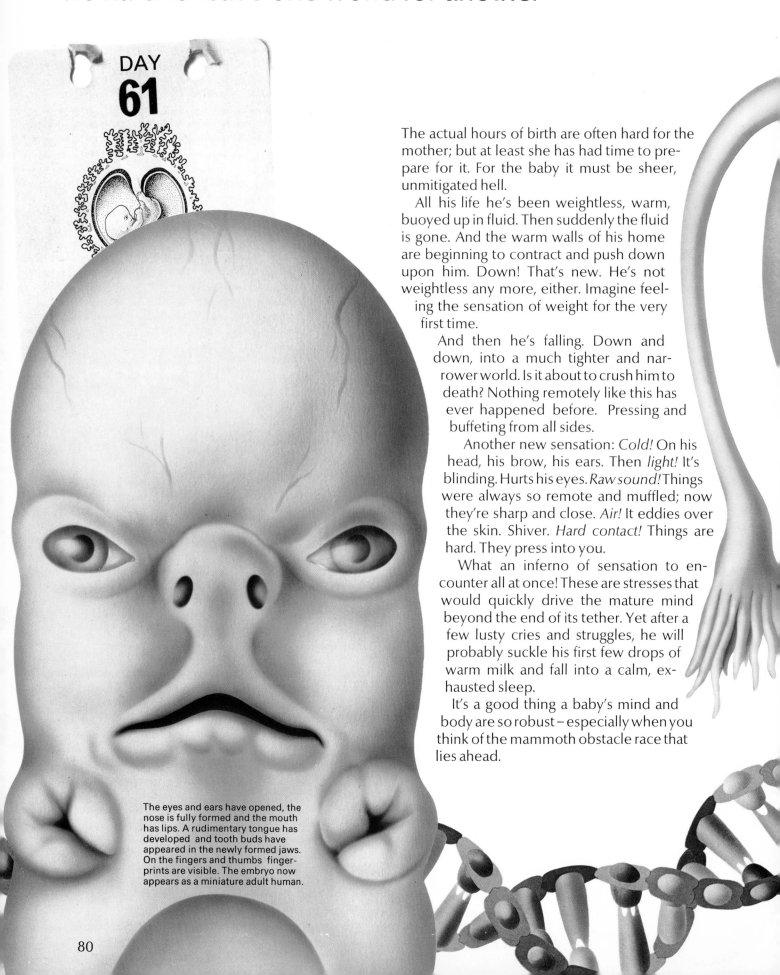

DAY
61

The eyes and ears have opened, the nose is fully formed and the mouth has lips. A rudimentary tongue has developed and tooth buds have appeared in the newly formed jaws. On the fingers and thumbs fingerprints are visible. The embryo now appears as a miniature adult human.

The actual hours of birth are often hard for the mother; but at least she has had time to prepare for it. For the baby it must be sheer, unmitigated hell.

All his life he's been weightless, warm, buoyed up in fluid. Then suddenly the fluid is gone. And the warm walls of his home are beginning to contract and push down upon him. Down! That's new. He's not weightless any more, either. Imagine feeling the sensation of weight for the very first time.

And then he's falling. Down and down, into a much tighter and narrower world. Is it about to crush him to death? Nothing remotely like this has ever happened before. Pressing and buffeting from all sides.

Another new sensation: *Cold!* On his head, his brow, his ears. Then *light!* It's blinding. Hurts his eyes. *Raw sound!* Things were always so remote and muffled; now they're sharp and close. *Air!* It eddies over the skin. Shiver. *Hard contact!* Things are hard. They press into you.

What an inferno of sensation to encounter all at once! These are stresses that would quickly drive the mature mind beyond the end of its tether. Yet after a few lusty cries and struggles, he will probably suckle his first few drops of warm milk and fall into a calm, exhausted sleep.

It's a good thing a baby's mind and body are so robust – especially when you think of the mammoth obstacle race that lies ahead.

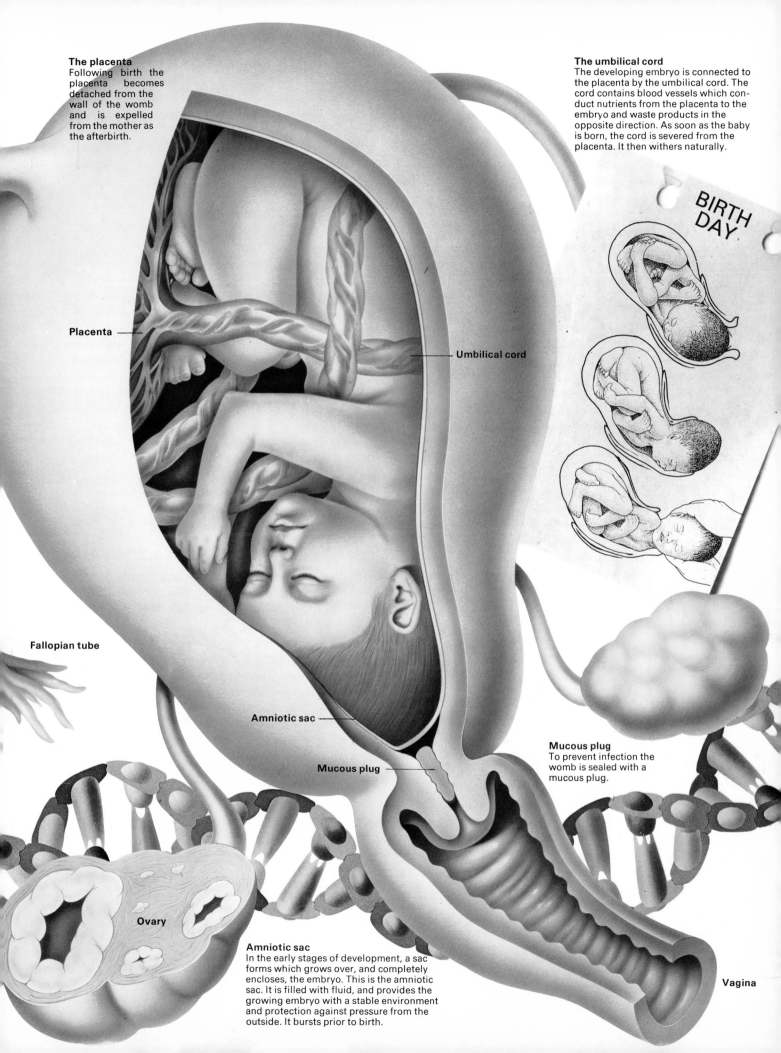

The placenta
Following birth the placenta becomes detached from the wall of the womb and is expelled from the mother as the afterbirth.

The umbilical cord
The developing embryo is connected to the placenta by the umbilical cord. The cord contains blood vessels which conduct nutrients from the placenta to the embryo and waste products in the opposite direction. As soon as the baby is born, the cord is severed from the placenta. It then withers naturally.

BIRTH DAY

Placenta

Umbilical cord

Fallopian tube

Amniotic sac

Mucous plug

Mucous plug
To prevent infection the womb is sealed with a mucous plug.

Ovary

Amniotic sac
In the early stages of development, a sac forms which grows over, and completely encloses, the embryo. This is the amniotic sac. It is filled with fluid, and provides the growing embryo with a stable environment and protection against pressure from the outside. It bursts prior to birth.

Vagina

With birth you discover chaos

The hell of new sensations that engulfed the baby at birth very soon gets organized in his mind. For human DNA builds a brain that is already programed to cope with exactly this sort of situation.

It all begins with the raw sensations. The touch of a mother's hands ... the taste of milk ... the smell of food ... the sounds of the hospital or household ... and a chaos of sights of ceilings and lights and faces. In the very beginning, too, there are sensations that *we* know are internal: the noise in your ears when you swallow ... the pleasant feeling of a full stomach ... the pain of wind ... the signals from your joints saying, for instance, your elbow is bent or your arm is straight. We cannot be certain a baby's mind makes any distinction between external and internal sensation. All we know is that various receptors – eyes, ears, nose, taste buds, hot-and-cold nerves, nerves of touch and internal feelings – all convert the sensations into tiny electrical impulses that travel along millions of nerve fibers and discharge their energy into the billions of cells of the brain.

We know, too, that the brain is already wired up like a computer, in the form of a pattern-recognition system. But it is more than a computer – at least, more than any computer we can imagine ourselves being able to build, now or in any forseeable future. For the brain sorts out the chaos of raw sensations into patterns, which it uses to recognize simple patterns in the outside world; it then sorts the simple patterns into superpatterns. Then it can go on to recognize the superpatterns in the outside world, and sort them into hyperpatterns ... and on and still on through increasing levels of order, never resting, never saying "task completed."

First of all the baby's brain has to *learn* to see. He's surrounded by radiation, from radio waves to cosmic rays. But he will never be able to sense the high-energy cosmic rays which plunge from outer space through the atmosphere, through him and on into the earth; he will never be aware of the radio waves which pass through him, leaving no mark on his consciousness. Only the narrow band of the spectrum that we call visible light awakens the nerves in his eyes. (Another tiny part of the spectrum registers on his skin as heat.)

Some groups of his eyes' light-sensitive cells are already cross-linked and then wired back into the brain in such a way that they respond to vertical lines; others to horizontal lines ... to sloping lines ... to movement this way ... that way ... and so on. All these groups need practice. And then those nerves have to be coordinated with the nerves that tell the eye muscles when, where, and how much to move. A lot of learning – but always using patterns out there in the real world as raw material.

His brain is being flooded with information. He hears a thrush singing at the window; he feels the fur and warmth of a cat; he smells a rose held beneath his nose. He doesn't yet know that it is a thrush or a cat or a rose; what he does know is that he hears and feels and smells. His DNA has seen to that. Somehow he has to sort out this information from the multitude of other impulses which are being volleyed to his brain.

Is there anywhere an end to this voyage of sensory discovery? None is in sight. The universe is full of exciting discoveries, each its own reward. As he begins to manipulate the immediate world – all in fun – his brain goes on picking up strands of data and weaving them into patterns of ideas. He pushes things away ... pulls them close ... lifts them ... feels them ... drops them ... yells, and notes who comes ... smiles, and gets cuddled ... babbles, and feels and hears how lips and tongue modulate the sound. And all the while, information about these and every other activity pours in through ears and eyes, tongue and muscles and skin, adding to the patterns, confirming some, destroying some, uniting others, making superpatterns.

Radiation

Cosmic ray

Chaos inside and outside
A newborn baby can see, hear, smell and feel,
but he cannot think. His optical and other
sensory centers are functioning, but the
front part of his brain cannot yet organize
the continuous jumble of sensations.

Heat

Sound

Light

Smell

83

You organize the world in your head

He grows. At the beginning he existed in an elementary world, the world dictated by his DNA, a world that lacked subtlety of meaning, although form and shape were there from the beginning. As he grows, he learns to embellish his primitive world with meaning and significance. He learns about shapes and colors and feelings. He learns to recognize articles and to use tools and objects. The original patterns that were formed in his brain soon after birth and during his first year of life become the filters through which he creates his own internal world.

But until he can speak and understand, his skill and intelligence are very similar to those of a baby chimpanzee of the same age; in fact, because a baby chimp is physically much more mature at birth, a human baby lags behind to start with. But sometime between his second and third year he makes the transition to a new land where no chimpanzee can follow: the land of language.

Of course he has started using words, singly and in simple groups, even earlier; but to do that he does not need to use his uniquely human intelligence. From his first weeks in the womb, his DNA has led him along the evolutionary trail from fish to man; here is its ultimate step. He develops that kind of intelligence that marks off man from all other living creatures: sequential intelligence.

The left half of his brain becomes the seat of the new sequential intelligence, the part that can cope with logical notions and complex sentences, one idea after another, strings of words or numbers. The right half is the center where ideas and patterns are handled, where the image is not broken down into parts and pieces but is seen whole. With this holistic side of the brain the baby assesses the size and shape of objects and how they relate to one another in space.

Here too is where he finds the way to a friend's house, or to school, or to a path through a wood . . . the thousands of mental maps we all of us use in our minds are there. He recognizes faces with this holistic half, too; and through it he comes to appreciate music.

These two halves work in perfect support of each other. Each contributes a different element to a child's intelligence; and both play a role in helping him sort out the world and his place within it.

Between them his two intelligences can soon process data from a vast number of sources that are just not available to other animals–books, for instance, and television, and above all talk with grown-ups and friends his own age. It is an unending process of interacting with the world and observing it.

In girls his own age the sequential brain is quicker to develop. They are better at languages and at seeing a logical point or connection. But around the age of 13 he will begin to catch up.

In the child's first decade it is almost all learning – running, jumping, climbing, swimming, to learn how well his body works; being naughty, to learn how far the rules may be stretched; playing mothers and fathers, or cops and robbers, or dwargs and martians, to learn what it might be like *not* to be himself; reading, asking questions, eavesdropping, to learn about a world beyond his own immediate experience; making up stories, listening to fairy tales, reading the funnies, to compare this world with the lands of never-was.

This is the time when the very basic patterns of his personality are laid down. It is when he learns to play the basic social roles which he will need when he grows up. Since the age of three, he has known that he is a boy and this information about his sexual identity, his core gender, is something which can never be removed from him. It is not a time of great rebellion. His self is yet too little to be very self assertive. He understands too little of the world to feel confident enough to want to change it.

But all that time, the self is growing, and the confidence is growing with it. Soon it will be time to apply all that learning and understanding.

Sequential

Holistic

Language helps to organize
Now sight and the other senses are well-developed and an understanding of language is beginning to form. Sequential intelligence is growing on the left, holistic on the right.

You organize the world outside

By the time he reaches his teens his two kinds of intelligence have amassed enough material to start building a new kind of inner world.

This impulse gets powerful support from the physical changes that occur. The sex cells begin to function, making sperms in boys and maturing the eggs in girls. The boy's voice deepens, facial and body hair sprouts, his frame expands and supports more powerful muscle. Girls his age develop breasts and fuller hips as well as pubic hair.

Mentally and physically, then, both become more like adults – yet not enough like them to fully join the adult world. It is an awkward time this, straddling the world of the child and the world of the adult. A turbulent time, when experiments and failures and false starts must all be got through before more lasting values can be found. Ideas and life styles are tried on like clothes – "does it suit me?" Undying friendships form that last a summer and yet are more intense than many that will come later and last longer. Pleasure is sought as if there were no tomorrow; and the exquisite sensations of self-sacrifice and denial are pursued relentlessly.

The adolescent spends these years becoming involved with ideas and causes, and seeking to find out who he is, what he stands for and where he comes from. This inner world is no longer the tell-me-a-story fantasy world of the junior; it is very real and uniquely his.

And it is unique because there never has been before, and never will be again, exactly his combination of DNA, unless he has an identical twin. And even then, his second line of inheritance – his cultural heritage – will be different.

But of course, not all the elements in his inner world are unique. Just as he holds most of his genes in common with all humans, so most of the elements of his new inner world are shared among everyone with the same cultural inheritance. But using his own unique gifts he will add to the common store – the cultural heritage – in some way. Maybe he will contribute brand new ideas or maybe refine old ones, making them more useful. They may not be narrowly intellectual ideas either; they could just as easily be in sport, music, engineering . . . politics . . . entertainment – the whole vast spectrum of human activity.

It is the new maturity of his brain which opens up these possibilities – a maturity built on at least 10 years interaction between his two kinds of intelligence. Simple ideas that he has learned can be used together with his experience to create elaborate concepts within his mind. One such idea might be that of rotation. When he was younger he gained a good bodily understanding of what "going round and round" means–wheels, merry-go-rounds, record players, gyroscopes and spinning till you're giddy.

Now those things add up to something more abstract and universal, concepts that include the movements of the planets, and ideas of rotation and time–even the sort of rotation that characterizes the helix of DNA. Beyond that he can tie in rotation with turning, with revolution, and with the most abstract ideas of revolution such as a radical change in art or science or politics.

In short, with the arrival of the adult human mind we have one more example of the original matter of the universe behaving in a new kind of way.

Before there was such a thing as the human mind, a new and beneficial mutation took generations to get established – and possibly much longer to become widespread. But with the human mind a new idea or a new technique or a new system can be established within years, or even less. In turn these new ideas or systems create a new world – a new environment – into which the next generation is born. This new world–this new cultural inheritance –they refine and to it they add their own store of ideas. Each new generation refining, adding, refining, adding...

Evolution has, in a way, shifted gear. Working through the mind and its brainchildren, rather than through DNA, it has both speeded up *and* vastly extended its scope.

A thinking individual
With 30 billion brain cells and all the basic
information for life, the brain is now complete.

So here you are . . .

So here you are, one complex and unique arrangement of that cosmic debris volleyed forth 15 billion years ago. Here you are at a moment when you are able to look at that debris, search for the patterns in it, organize them and possibly change them. This book unfolds one pattern. One day, any day, it may change; you may change it yourself. What makes you unique is that you are probably the only creature capable of recognizing the fact.

Let's look at the story again. Simple chemicals, washing around in a thin soup on a barren Earth, combining and breaking apart, haphazardly formed one combination that had the power to duplicate itself by consuming energy and molecules from the soup around it. We call the process *life*. And the combination is DNA. The same process, working over the last three billion years has produced the countless species, living and extinct, that make up the pageant of life on Earth: random change in the DNA . . . little pockets and backwaters where unexploited opportunities give the newcomer its chance to get established in a small way . . . then the fierce competition to survive in the large, stable systems which determines whether the newcomer remains a rare oddball or joins the big time – or simply vanishes altogether.

The result has been two quite different kinds of progress. One has led toward perfect adaptation to a particular set of conditions; bacteria that thrive only in certain near-boiling waterholes . . . molds that grow only in jet fuel tanks . . . fish that can exist only in subterranean waters . . . plants and molluscs that need hot, alkali mud. These are but a few of literally thousands of marvelously adapted specialist creatures. The other kind of improvement is the very opposite. It shuns all specialization, all extremes. Instead it centers on all-round general advances of the kind that fit plants and animals to make better use of almost any environment.

These advances are what you could call the main stream of evolution. They run the whole gamut, from the ability to trap the sun's energy, through the ability to move . . . to form multi-celled creatures . . . the development of the through-tube gut instead of a sack-type gut . . . blood systems . . . nerve systems

. . . skeletons . . . eyesight, touch and other senses . . . survival out of water . . . warm bloodedness . . . increased intelligence . . . toolmaking . . . the power of speech . . . civilization.

There is something odd about that list. It outlines a steady progress in the general development of living things; each advance helps its possessors to survive globally, not just in this or that special environment. It marks a steady line of increasing complexity and sophistication, culminating in human intelligence and its consequences. These consequences are the last three items on the list: toolmaking, the power of speech, civilization. They are also the oddities, for they are not specified by the DNA. They are like a torch that must be tended and passed on from generation to generation. They are our cultural inheritance.

With the emergence of man, evolution took a sudden lurch in a new direction. For almost three billion years it had been an accidental and automatic process, following its own built-in laws of self-improvement. Then, suddenly, came man. For most of our two to three million years on Earth, our intelligence merely helped us stay one step ahead of extinction. But with the invention of agriculture and the building of civilization leading to the latter-day discoveries of science, things really acquired lift-off. And it began only about ten thousand years ago. "Suddenly" is really too leisurely a word to describe it.

Imagine life is just 12 hours old. It began around breakfast time, eight o'clock say, and now it's coming up to eight in the evening. There are 43,200 seconds in that span; man appears in the last 12 of them; civilization and the dawn of recorded history occupy the last *tenth* of the last second.

The Earth must have seen many remarkable moments during its long life, but the most remarkable has to be this latest, briefest twist to the tale – the moment when that sizzling matter, hurled outward from the Big Bang, finally organized in such a configuration as to become aware of itself. And then went on to dig out the whole amazing story.

What makes it even more amazing is that so far as we know this awareness is unique. True, there are

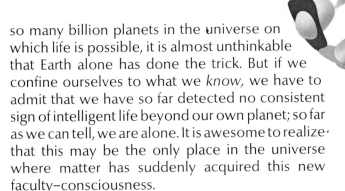

so many billion planets in the universe on which life is possible, it is almost unthinkable that Earth alone has done the trick. But if we confine ourselves to what we *know,* we have to admit that we have so far detected no consistent sign of intelligent life beyond our own planet; so far as we can tell, we are alone. It is awesome to realize· that this may be the only place in the universe where matter has suddenly acquired this new faculty–consciousness.

If we confine ourselves to what we *know,* we also have to confess that the story unfolded in this book is not the whole truth. For the sort of truth we are dealing with here can never be considered final. There is always room to improve the detail of what we already think we know. And, even more important and exciting, every new discovery opens up further areas of bewilderment.

No one saw the Big Bang, or the fragments of the prototype universe flying apart, or the gas slowly circling and condensing into the stars and planets. No one was around when the Earth began to heat up to melting point and then cool into different crystalline layers. No one observed the molecules drifting and linking in the early "soup". So why are we convinced that this particular sequence of events is, in the light of our present incomplete knowledge, the most likely?

· Take the Big Bang, for instance. The evidence for that comes from our experience of how atomic particles behave in giant atom-smashing machines, from measurements of the light from distant galaxies, which show them moving away, and observations of the radio waves that form the general background radiation of space, which suggest that there was an enormous explosion billions of years ago. The theory that most adequately links up these diverse events in one single explanation is, at present, the Big Bang theory. But that doesn't guarantee its truth; and there are astronomers who argue that other explanations are at least possible. So be prepared to hear that the Big Bang theory has been replaced by some other idea that offers an even better and more comprehensive explanation of the known facts.

Other parts of the story, however, rest on much firmer evidence. Take evolution. The theory was first put forward by Charles Darwin in 1859. Every observation since then has only made it seem more likely. We have even been able to watch a speeded-up version of simple evolution at work in the laboratory – remember Stanley Miller's experiment? And with the discovery of the components of DNA – made as recently as 1953 by Francis Crick and James D. Watson – we can add a step-by-step explanation of its mechanism. So it would be very surprising if evolutionary theory were ever to be replaced by some quite different explanation. But that does not mean that all the details are now final. We can, for example, still only make an intelligent guess at precisely what happened in the "soup."

So this book offers one explanation that can be said to fit our present state of knowledge and the observable facts. It has many predecessors, right back to our earliest records. All of them have been wrong in part. Some of the patterns they claimed to see simply vanished when we came to look a little more closely. Many of their "final" discoveries turned into mere beachheads to a vast new hinterland of knowledge. Problems that they considered forever insoluble have long since ceased to perplex even our youngest students of science.

Is this book any different? Of course not. Centuries from now most teenagers, if they happened to glance through any surviving copies of it, would soon find a dozen places to smile at our ignorance. Perhaps something that you will do during your lifetime will help put that smile there. Perhaps something reported in this book – something you disagree with or think very doubtful – will have started you on that work.

Why was there anything at all?

Ever since people first realized that the stars are not of this world, but in some remote, other-worldly sphere, far beyond the reach of slingshot or arrow, beyond all our senses except that of vision - ever since then we have asked "why?"

The question is so insistent that we dare not leave it unanswered. And each generation has answered it in terms that best fit everything else it knows of life and the world. So: the stars are the eyes of the spirits ... the adornment of a Great King's raiment ... a portent of the future, if only we learn to read their movements properly ... For most of our history we have silenced that question with answers like those.

The one thing we did not dare to say was: "We don't know. Let's try to find out." In fact, we had not the vaguest idea of how to start finding out. Those answers, because they were final, closed off all further inquiry.

Then a few hundred years ago, just after a few bold navigators and sea captains from Europe had shown that the world was very different from all previous conceptions of it, all sorts of people began to see advantages in admitting their ignorance and saying those challenging words: "Let's try to find out." It was the birth of modern science.

Today we grow up with this new outlook. When we make a personal discovery our first question is: "Does it fit in with our present theories – or am I into something new?" We would actually feel more excited if the discovery completely demolished some existing belief rather than upheld it. We find it hard to realize how very new this attitude is. Most of the people who have ever lived would certainly think it dangerous and probably insane. Their first question would have been: "Quick – how can this discovery be made to fit our present theories?"

Yet there are those fundamental *why* questions to which we cannot answer: "Let's find out." There is no way of finding out. But who, reading the story of life's development from a mixture of soup and crystals and gas, seeing it unfold in all its marvelous detail, who can fail to be stirred with wonder, stirred into asking that unanswerable why? Why did it happen? Why was there anything at all?

This is not a question about the mechanism of the universe; questions about mechanisms always take us back to the dead-end of an observable fact. For instance, the question "why is water wet?" takes us swiftly back through a chain of mechanisms until we reach the statement: "It is an observable fact that hydrogen and oxygen, combined in this way, form a molecule with such and such properties." If you still ask "why?" you are going beyond mechanism into the realms of purpose. So when we ask "why?" about the universe we are asking what is its purpose.

A purpose implies a conclusion of some kind, an achievement, an end. So if the universe has a purpose, it also has an end: the moment when the purpose is achieved. In other words, when you ask, "Why does the universe exist?" your question assumes that the universe has an end.

In that case, it is no use asking scientists for an answer – or anybody who gets his answers by studying the measurable, touchable, visible, physical, chemical world – because nobody has yet found any conclusive evidence that this universe *can* come to an end. And even if it does, there is no law which dictates that an end implies a purpose.

True, this particular arrangement of the matter within it will change. If gravity wins its fight to reverse the expansion of the universe, the matter of the universe will cease traveling outward about 25 billion years from now and will then spend a further 40 billion years retracing its path until it all collapses in upon one point, where it will turn into ... the thing-we-have-no-name-for. If it then starts all over, that will be because it is its very nature to do so; it could no more help starting over than water can "help" being wet. To a cosmic observer – a creature of pure consciousness, devoid of matter and therefore able to stay outside the material universe while it collapsed – our why-purpose question would have turned into a why-mechanism question, and it would have run into the customary dead-end of observable fact. But *we* would never be able to observe it. We would merely have to take his word (or, as some would spell it, His Word) for it. Whether such a being could answer in terms intelligible to creatures imprisoned in space and time is quite another matter.

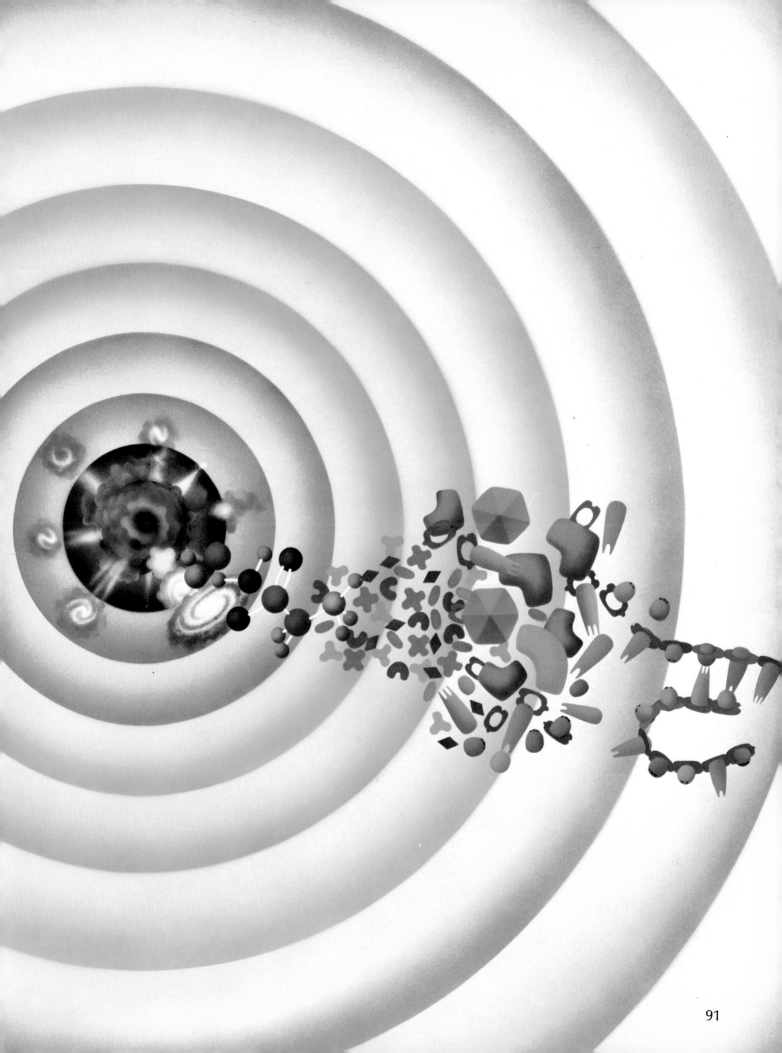

Life constantly works toward a crisis

When we notice something happening "out there" in the world and see that it has a developing pattern, we automatically apply that understanding to answer the question: "What next?" We cannot help doing it, either in small things (Will I be able to cross the road before the car comes?) or in big things (Is the increasing hostility between the nations going to lead to war?). Now that we have noticed a pattern in our evolution, and have even discovered the basic mechanism of the process, can we use this to help predict where we are going?

The blunt answer is: No. Not if we seek for some kind of inevitable future that will happen come what may. If the story of evolution tells us anything, it teaches that chance…accident…luck – whatever you prefer to call it – has played a major role at each new stage. Even the perfection of a rose owes its existence to chance. And so too does the human brain with its staggering ability to probe its own origins, to create gods and beauty and machines. Looking back through evolution we may discern patterns that appear inevitable; but that is only because we can now see the logical connection between earlier and later events.

But if we are looking for likelihoods rather than certainties, the story of evolution is packed with helpful clues.

In the first place we can see that despite its furious bustle, life is basically lazy. It always takes the easiest path on offer. If there's lots of food around, as there was in the primitive soup, living things use it; they don't go to the extra trouble of making it for themselves. That doesn't become necessary until there is a crisis in the food supply. *Then* comes the appropriate mutation – with luck.

Life constantly works toward a crisis. It paints itself into a corner and then, when it seems there is no way out, along comes a change in the DNA that is the equivalent of changing the architecture of the building. The corner is no longer a corner, the paintbrush is now in new hands, and we are off again for the next corner, the next crisis.

Humanity is approaching such a crisis now. It is amazingly similar to the one that primitive life faced when the ready-made foods in the soup began to run out. Our "soup" is the Earth's crust, a storehouse of raw materials for our kind of civilization. We now depend totally on that supply of fuels and minerals to sustain us. The difference is that the crisis for life in the early soup resulted from the kind of DNA that was then found in living things; but ours is not so directly connected with our DNA. Our crisis is the result of our *other* kind of inheritance: cultural evolution. It is our civilization rather than life itself which is directly at stake, but the two are nevertheless very closely interwoven.

We are in this plight because we used our brains, realized the potential value of the raw materials and fuels in the Earth around us, and then did the easiest thing possible – which was to use them up just as fast as we wanted. So the "mutation" that will (with luck – always with luck) get us out of the corner we have painted ourselves into, will not be of the DNA kind; it will be a "mutation" in our pattern of cultural evolution and it will depend on our using our brains once more.

But the lesson from the primitive soup still holds, however different the "mutation" may be in character. When all the easily available supplies ran out, living things had to turn to the only steady, regular, reliable source of energy this earth has ever known, and they had to tap that energy in order to make fresh supplies–in their case of food. Not only that–living things then had to find a way of bringing the whole process into balance, so that as fast as atoms of carbon, hydrogen and oxygen were knit up into sugars they were broken back again into water and carbon dioxide ready for re-use, again and again and again. Life had to find the trick of recycling the materials it was going to put to such constant use.

It will be the same for us. The primitive soup got its energy from the sun, of course – and remember that the sun radiates towards Earth two million times mankind's present energy requirement. So we must find some direct way of tapping that energy. Indeed, we have probably already found it. There are literally hundreds of groups around the world now working on this one problem.

In short, we have no insoluble energy problem. We have no insoluble food problem. We also know how to recycle all our other raw materials; at the moment, the supply from the Earth's crust is still too plentiful, and so the materials are still too cheap to make recycling a rewarding enough process. But when the supply really runs scarce, recycling will take over.

We maybe have a population problem, in that there is a difference between the numbers of people that the Earth can support and the (much smaller) numbers that would make for a pleasant existence for everyone. But that problem is not insoluble either. And if enough people decide that smaller would be more beautiful – we already have highly effective birth control methods. We really face no problems that – using our present cultural inheritance – we cannot solve.

But our very immediate future may not be pleasant. We can take no pride in acknowledging that, to judge by our past record, it will probably take a great deal of death and misery to convince us of the need to give up old and familiar routines and take up new-fangled ones instead. But again evolution shows us that this cruel form of progress is almost as old as life itself; our own human evolution shows that we can quickly re-cover even from the most terrible ordeals.

Where am I going to?

What, then, of the long-term future? Assuming we stabilize our material problems, what is the next likely step in our development? As long as we are dealing with relatively short periods in evolutionary terms–say, less than a million years–it will be a development based on cultural inheritance rather than on DNA.

Again, we can see a clear pattern emerging. In the beginning the whole Earth, depended on the interplay of vast quantities of energy over a huge length of time. Energy is still vital to life, but since those days we have seen a steady increase in the effectiveness with which it is used. You may remember how the change from fermentation to oxygen breathing yielded 19 times as much energy from the same foodstuffs? That was just one step along the way. The human brain was another great leap forward, for it uses only a few watts of energy. Yet its potential is so vast as to be incalculable. Now we can glimpse the beginnings of other changes which may make an even more profound impact on our use of energy. It is all to do with our handling of information.

Remember how the emergence of language enabled us to impart and receive information of increasing complexity. Writing was the next momentous breakthrough, for this information could now be stored *outside* the human body. And now information can be stored in huge quantities on tiny magnetic tapes, and it can be flashed around the world in seconds. The societies of the future will be based on more and more information being exchanged with less and less wastage of time and energy. This ever-increasing complexity of information will alter our cultural inheritance changing the way we behave, the way we live, even the way we think.

We are even looking again at the original information store, the DNA molecule. We are beginning to eye it as a painter looks at a box of paints. Can we alter a DNA molecule so that it will build whatever we program it to–from food to computers to a new kind of human who can live on another planet, in another solar system, in another galaxy? Already there are experiments afoot to change some of the simplest forms of DNA–those in bacteria–in ways unknown in nature. It will probably be many decades, before we can produce any particular effect we want. But now that we know it is chemically possible to change individual genes, what is going to stop a creature with our curiosity and love of experiment from attempting just that?

And what is then going to stop us from spreading outward, seeding the stars with life? Would that not be a direct continuation of everything that has happened before? Even if we are the only intelligences in the universe–what can stop us from filling it, rim to shining rim?

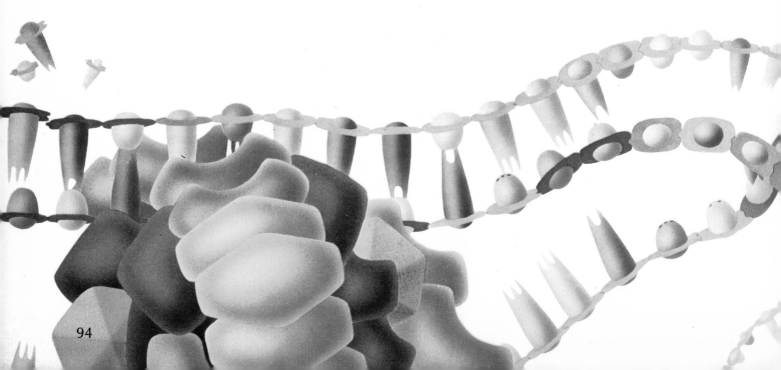